98°

THE OFFICIAL BOOK

BY 98° WITH K.M. SQUIRES

books

*For my husband, Ronnie Rodriguez,
con mucho amor— K.M.S.*

An original publication of
MTV BOOKS/ POCKET BOOKS
Copyright ©1999 by 98 Degrees Music, Inc.
All rights reserved, including the right
to reproduce this book or portions thereof
in any form whatsoever. For information
address Pocket Books, 1230 Avenue of the
Americas, New York, NY 10020

POCKET BOOKS, a division of Simon &
Schuster, Inc. 1230 Avenue of the Americas,
New York, NY 10020

POCKET and colophon are registered
trademarks of Simon & Schuster, Inc.

Copyright ©1999 by 98 Degrees Music, Inc.
All rights reserved.

MTV Music Television and all related titles,
logos, and characters are trademarks of
MTV Networks, a division of Viacom
International Inc.

All photographs credited to Julie Blattberg
are copyright ©1999 Julie Blattberg.

All photographs courtesy of THE WALT
DISNEY COMPANY are copyright ©1999
THE WALT DISNEY COMPANY.

Cover photograph ©1999 98 Degrees
Music, Inc., under License from
PolyGram Merchandising, Inc.

Cover photograph by Marina Chavez.

ISBN: 0-671-04169-X

10 9 8 7 6 5 4 3 2 1

First MTV Books/Pocket Books
trade paperback printing September 1999

Printed in the U.S.A.

Acknowledgments:
K.M. Squires wishes to thank the following
for their generous support and hard work:
Ingrid van der Leeden, Julie Blattberg,
Rodger Weinfeld, and everyone at Pocket
Books; everyone at MTV; everyone at
Universal Records; Christine Squires for her
invaluable help; Paris D'Jon, Johnny
Camisa, Melissa Casalino, and everyone at
Top 40 Entertainment; and especially the
guys and their families for their cooperation:
Nick, Jeff, Justin, and Drew—thanks for
making my job easy and so much fun.

For orders other than by individual consumers, Pocket Books grants a discount
on the purchase of 10 or more copies of single titles for special markets or premium
use. For further details, please write to the
Vice-President of Special Markets, Pocket
Books, 1633 Broadway, New York, NY
10019-6785, 8th Floor.

For information on how individual consumers
can place orders, please write to Mail
Order Department, Simon & Schuster
Inc., 100 Front Street, Riverside, New
Jersey 08075.

**For all of our fans.
Thank you for
always being there.
You're the best!**

CONTENTS

Marina Chavez

Johnny Camisa

What do you get when you mix four talented singers with heart-melting harmonies, healthy good looks, and intense dedication to their dreams? The answer is Nick Lachey, 25, a well-mannered Midwestern boy and a second tenor full of sweet soul; Jeff Timmons, 26, a warm and friendly first tenor who loves to laugh; Drew Lachey, 23, a baritone brimming with ideas and energy; and Justin Jeffre, 26, a laid-back, good-natured guy with a booming bass. They are the vocal group 98°, which is currently burning up the *Billboard* charts with its own special soulful blend of pop and R&B.

Four years ago this Ohio born-and-bred quartet packed up and moved to Los Angeles with little more than a few dollars and a dream. They took on odd jobs, from dishwashing to security to delivering Chinese food, and sang wherever they could get noticed.

Their persistence paid off when they grabbed the attention of a hotshot manager after working their way backstage at a Boyz II Men concert. Less than six months after being discovered, the guys snagged a record deal with famous recording label Motown Records.

Their careers quickly heated up. With two scorching albums under their belts—the latest, *98° And Rising*, certified platinum—there was nowhere to go but the top for this awesome foursome. But as the guys will tell you, getting there wasn't always easy.

Get up close and personal with the four down-to-earth, gifted, all-American guys behind it all. Turn the page and discover why 98° is raising body temperatures all over the globe. Find out how they got together, why they are not like other vocal groups, how they feel about fame and their fans, and what is going on in their love lives. Here is their story in their own words, in the only *official* biography of the hottest group in the music scene today: 98°.

*I*t wasn't easy putting together the burning hot vocal group 98°. Just ask Jeff Timmons, the man who started it all. "With a lot of coaxing I finally convinced some friends of mine to come out to L.A. and form a band with me," he says. But these particular friends were not current bandmates Drew Lachey, Nick Lachey, and Justin Jeffre. "I didn't know Drew, Nick, or Justin from Ohio at all. They were recommended to me by a friend after the original guys quit," Jeff explains. "I never really let the burning desire to form a vocal group die, even after my friends quit. I placed ads in the papers, and interviewed maybe two dozen people, and had them sing for me. But I wasn't having any luck. It was through my brother's roommate's manager that the first good connection was made. She introduced me to this guy Jon, who had gone to school with Nick, Justin, and Drew."

Jeff continues, "Jon and I started singing together. One day he said, 'I know this guy, Nick. He's good-looking and has a lot of talent.' At that point I wasn't ready to give up, so I called him and when I talked to him he seemed really cool. I heard him

In the studio recording the demo, with Montell Jordan.

were trying to save our money, and Boyz II Men tickets were expensive," Justin remembers. "Nick and Jeff didn't want to go because it was expensive and there was a big football game on, so Jon and I had to convince them to go. Once we got there we tried to go backstage and sing, and there was this girl who was listening to us. It turned out that she worked for a local radio station that was hosting the concert. She made us sing in front of a crowd and said,

'If you can impress this crowd we will put you on the radio.' The crowd liked it and Paris heard us."

"I was walking backstage and I heard these voices harmonizing,"

sing 'In the Still of the Night' on the phone and he wanted to hear us sing, too, so we sang a Boyz II Men song. That convinced Nick. I feel like fate guided us together in a weird way."

That was 1995. Although he was wary at first, Nick trusted his friend Jon's judgment and drove across the country to L.A. Nick was out there only a few weeks when he suggested they bring in his pal, Justin Jeffre from Cincinnati, as a bass.

Even though he was studying history and political science at the University of Cincinnati, Justin was waiting for this type of opportunity. In a flash he too left the Midwest for Tinseltown.

Nick, Jon, Jeff, and Justin worked odd jobs during the day

and sang wherever and whenever they could as a group called Just Us. Because of their persistence, they were able to land a gig, one

of their first, in Dodger Stadium singing the national anthem, even though they were unknowns. Their determination to get backstage at a Boyz II Men concert caused them to hit the jackpot. While there, they caught the attention of their current manager, Paris D'Jon, who has worked with pop sensations Montell Jordan, Foxy Brown, LL Cool J, and C&C Music Factory.

"When we first moved out we

"I WAS WALKING BACKSTAGE AND I HEARD THESE VOICES HARMONIZING. I WAS VERY IMPRESSED..."
— Manager Paris D'Jon, the man who discovered 98°'s sound.

Paris recalls. "I was very impressed, and I started talking to them. They told me they were trying to meet Boyz II Men, and I told them that was not going to happen, because Boyz II Men were getting ready to jump in the van. But I did tell them that I liked their sound and that I was really interested, and I signed them a couple of months later."

"There weren't any groups out at that time that had that type

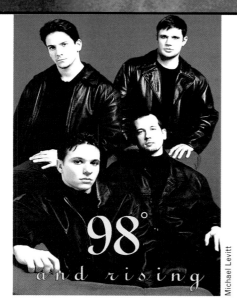

An early promo piece for 98°

of sound, except for Boyz II Men," Paris points out. "This was the first white group that really sounded pop, and I thought there was a great marketing opportunity there."

Paris hooked the foursome up with a gig at L.A.'s House of Blues to open for Montell Jordan. But right before the gig, Jon decided that his heart was really in acting, and he quit the group. The guys were stuck. They had an important show coming up in a few weeks and they needed a baritone.

Nick came to the rescue. He called his younger brother, Drew, who was living in Brooklyn and working as an EMT. Even though Drew enjoyed life on the East Coast, he had always felt he was a performer at heart. At his brother's request, he quit his job, packed his bags, and drove out West.

Drew proved to be the perfect addition to the group. "I think our voices really blend well and have a distinct, smooth sound that's R&B with some funk and soul," Nick says. "That's not something you often get when you put four people together."

"We had a good chemistry with our personalities and vocal styles," Justin says. "But chemistry in personalities is even more important than vocal chemistry. The day that Drew joined the group it was like we knew it was something special and very unique."

Although the sound fit, the guys weren't particularly happy with the name Just Us. Adding a new member gave them the perfect opportunity to change it. "Deciding on the name was a group thing," Drew explains. "We had a bunch of names that we really didn't like, like Next Issue and Inertia. Somehow 98° got thrown out there, and we kind of liked it because of the whole body temperature thing and we were singing a lot of love songs. We felt that 98° created an atmosphere of heat and passion and romance that's appropriate to our sound. You have to admit, whether you love or hate it, you remember it."

So now they had the lineup, the name, the manager, and the sound. All they needed was a record label. "From there, Paris helped us get a demo together," Jeff explains.

"When I put the demo together," recalls Paris, "I hired Jimmy 'Professor Funk' Russell to produce it for me—he was a bass player for Montell. He went into the studio every night with the guys. At the same time the guys were rehearsing with a choreographer, Kim Morrow, in her living room, during the day, and recording at night. Once the demo was done, I went to Montell and said I wanted to do two more songs. I then got a guy named Sean 'Mystro' Mathers, a DJ out of D.C., to do the last two songs. Montell produced those last two songs with him. It was a big collaboration. Then we packed this baby up and sent it to tons of record companies, and got about five callbacks. I also gave the tape to one of Montell's dancers, Hi-Hat. She gave it to Clark Kent, the V.P. at Motown. He called me up and said, 'Listen, Andre Harrell is the new president of Motown and he really likes the sound of the guys.' Then Andre got on the phone and said, 'You've got to get these guys in here tomorrow.' The guys lived in L.A. and I was in New York. I got on a plane that day, flew to L.A., and after he heard the guys' incredible sound right in front of him, he signed them on the spot. Other labels heard the demo, and they liked it, but we never got a chance to meet with anybody else, because of the immediate response and commitment from Motown."

The guys couldn't believe their luck. Just six months after they had formed, a record label was taking them seriously. And it wasn't just any record label. It was Motown Records, a label that had literally invented a whole sound.

"When we went in to sing for the president of Motown, we were very nervous," Jeff continues.

"He asked us if we could dance, and fortunately we had been working with a choreographer for a week. I'm still having trouble dancing, and I was terrible that day, but somehow we made it through. Then we sang for him, and he loved it. Just like that, he said, 'I want to sign you.'"

The group was amazed that the label that was home to such superstars as Diana Ross and the Supremes, the Temptations, the Jacksons, and Stevie Wonder had signed them. "It was like a dream," Jeff says. "When I pictured how I wanted it to turn out, and when it turned out the way I envisioned it, it was extra freaky. We always talked about Motown, that we

wanted to be the first white guys on Motown, singing harmony-based pop music and all that. It's amazing that it actually turned out that way."

"Honestly, we didn't even think we had a chance at Motown," Drew says incredulously. "They're historically a black label and we really didn't think they would be interested in a white group from Ohio. But when we heard that they wanted to sign us we were in shock because they have such an amazing legacy of great artists. They were our dream label. Everything was coming together at a time when it seemed that we were really on our way, that we had a legitimate chance of making it and that this wasn't just some pipe dream. We realized that our dreams could come true."

Drew, Nick, Jeff, and Justin immediately set to work on their self-titled debut album, *98°*, with songs written and produced by the likes of buddy Montell Jordan and Atlanta-based R&B producers Tricky and Sean. It was recorded in New York, Atlanta, and Los Angeles and released in July 1997, less than two years after the band solidified.

"WE REALIZED THAT OUR DREAMS COULD COME TRUE."

Hangin' in Toronto.

Johnny Camisa

14°

Johnny Camisa

On tour in the Philippines.

opportunity was waiting for them. Motown wanted to pair the guys up with one of its major artists for a song on the soundtrack of the animated Disney blockbuster Mulan.

"Originally, they wanted us to do 'True to Your Heart' with the Temptations," Justin explains. "But when I heard the sample of the song, it reminded me of Stevie Wonder. We came up with the idea of having Stevie on it and it worked out perfectly."

riffs and singing harmony parts together," Nick says. "It was completely unreal."

When they filmed the video in Hollywood, they had their big chance to meet the superstar. "He came onto the video set and a hush fell," Drew remembers. "Everybody just got real quiet. It was like royalty came into the room. He was just really down-to-earth. He actually had his keyboard and computer set up in his trailer and he invited us in later and we had a little jam session. It was really amazing."

"I couldn't really believe it was happening," Nick gushes. "In retrospect I can appreciate how special that was, and how much he means to music and people. It was awesome. We did nothing to deserve that opportunity, and we were really blessed that it happened for us. It was

The first single, "Invisible Man," climbed as high as No.12 on the Billboard charts, and the song earned the group its first gold record.

Soon Justin, Jeff, Drew, and Nick were no longer invisible men. They filmed their first videos and embarked on tours of cheerleading camps, amusement parks, and malls. Things heated up on an overseas tour that yielded a frenetic fan following. They hit it bigger in Canada, Europe, and Asia than on their home turf. But mega-success in the States wasn't too far behind.

When 98° returned home, a rare

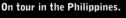

With Russell Simmons while filming the "Invisible Man" video.

Though the guys didn't meet Stevie while recording the song, they were still blown away by their chance to sing with him. "It was awesome to hear your voice with Stevie Wonder, exchanging

98° with Paris, receiving Hong Kong Channel V award for Multi-Platinum Best Boy Band CD.

Johnny Camisa

Live with Regis and Kathie Lee.

definitely a dream come true—something we will always remember."

"I am the biggest Stevie Wonder fan you'll ever meet," says Justin. "It was one of the most exciting experiences of my life. If it all ends tomorrow, it's something I always will remember and I consider it a great blessing. It just proves that dreams can come true."

"He was so down-to-earth it was unbelievable," Jeff adds. "Here you have a guy who is one of the most successful artists in music and he was more down-to-earth than someone I had just met performing at a radio show."

"True to Your Heart" was the first song the guys recorded for their second album, *98° and Rising*. They jetted from New York to Nashville to Los Angeles to Vancouver to meet up with some of the business's hottest producers, including the Trackmasters, (Mariah Carey, Will Smith, LL Cool J, and Mary J. Blige), who

Preparing to shoot the video "Because of You."

On the set of "Because of You."   Johnny Camisa

laid down the sample of Kool & the Gang's "Get Down on It" for "Do You Wanna Dance." The quartet also worked with Pras of the Fugees on "Fly With Me" and Anders Bagge of Robyn and Ace of Base fame on "Because of You."

The album also includes two well-chosen remakes. 98° teamed up with producer Keith Thomas (who has worked with Vanessa Williams and Brian McKnight) for the cover of the Mark Wills country hit "I Do (Cherish You)." The arrangement of Michael Jackson's "She's Out of My Life" from their demo tape also made the cut. The guys feel that they contributed more as producers and songwriters on the second album. "We definitely had a more hands-on approach for this album," Jeff points out.

How do four guys write one song? "Sometimes we start writing a song together, and other times, one person will start a song and he'll bring other guys in to brainstorm. Other times one person will write a whole song himself," Nick explains. "I think when we all write together we look for a creative theme, and we just try to find a collective understanding of where the song is coming from and where it's going. We've done it where every one of us has written a different part of the song and pieced it together. There really is no set formula."

A quiet moment on the beach during the shoot.
Johhny Camisa

16°

But isn't it hard to get four guys to agree on how one song should sound?

"Sometimes when not everyone agrees you have to have the old diplomacy in there and vote on it," Nick goes on. "Rock, paper, scissors is our backbone."

The effort was released in October 1998, right after Motown was absorbed by Universal Records. Universal supported the group just as much as Motown did, and soon they had a platinum album on their hands. The hit single "Because of You" raced up to No. 3 on the Billboard charts. "The Hardest Thing" followed quickly on its heels, zooming up the Top 20.

98° went on to film four videos for their second album, including "True to Your Heart," which gave them a memory they'll never forget in working with Stevie Wonder, and "I Do (Cherish You)." But if you ask the guys which videos were their favorites to make, they're torn between "Because of You," in which they got the best view of the Bay Area from atop the Golden Gate Bridge, or "The

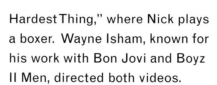

Johnny Lamus
98° on their way up — to the top of the Golden Gate Bridge in San Francisco.

Hardest Thing," where Nick plays a boxer. Wayne Isham, known for his work with Bon Jovi and Boyz II Men, directed both videos.

For "Because of You," Jeff had to conquer his lifelong fear of heights. "Getting on top of the bridge ended up being very cool," he says. "Not everyone gets to do something like that. We got to go up there and sing a song and it was a beautiful, clear day. It was a day I will never forget."

"I put a lot into 'The Hardest Thing,'" Nick says. "I trained hard for it on the physical side. And it was almost like acting again; it

was more than just standing and singing. It was a lot of fun to make, but it was a little painful for me because they kept spraying me down with this cold water bottle to make it look like I was sweating, and it was freezing in the studio!"

"I like 'The Hardest Thing' too," Drew seconds, "because it has a story line to it. Plus, it was filmed in Vegas, so when we were finished I got to go down to the slots and blackjack tables and lose my money!"

A publicity storm followed, and the guys were bombarded

with requests for appearances. They sang "True to Your Heart" with Stevie Wonder on *The Tonight Show* with Jay Leno, a definite highlight for the quartet. "That's the biggest adrenaline rush I've had since I've been doing this," Jeff says. "I couldn't help but think, 'What am I doing here?'"

They went on to perform at the Super Bowl, and Macy's

They filmed a concert for a pay-per-view special, have just wrapped a home video, and will release a Christmas album just in time for the '99 holiday season. Their third single from *98° And Rising*, "I Do," is included in the Julia Roberts/Hugh Grant film *Notting Hill*, and there's even talk of a Monkees-style sitcom starring the awesome foursome.

"YOU WOULD THINK THAT LIVING TOGETHER AFTER FOUR YEARS AND BEING WITH EACH OTHER ALL THE TIME WE WOULD BE SICK OF EACH OTHER. BUT WHEN WE HAVE TIME OFF WE STILL CALL EACH OTHER AND HANG OUT TOGETHER."

Thanksgiving Day Parade. Television appearances included *Live With Regis & Kathie Lee*, *Rosie O'Donnell*, *The View*, and *Today*, as well as Macy's Fourth of July fire works. They played themselves on the soap *As the World Turns* and the sitcom *City Guys*, and hosted *MTV's Spring Break '99.*

Their sold-out "Heat It Up" concert tour in the spring of '99 drew rave reviews, and the guys went on to headline Nickelodeon's "All That" tour with Monica and to tape the ABC-TV special Disney's "Summer Jam," at The Walt Disney World Resort.

What could they possibly do next? 98° has plenty in store.

Before they get to work on their next album, they'll take a well-deserved break, during which they'll visit their families, and surprisingly, spend time with one another. "It's kind of sick how much we hang out with each other," Drew says. "You would think that living together after four years and being with each other all the time we would be sick of each other. But when we have time off we still call each other and hang out and go to clubs together." He goes on to explain that the guys aren't just coworkers. "We are each other's family. We don't have family when we are on the road and our friends are all over the place, so we've all

98° And Rising goes platinum.

become each other's family."

Friendship, talent, and dedication make 98° hotter than any other pop group today. No doubt, that combination is the secret to their success.

Yeah, it's all "Because of You." On top of the world, filming from the Golden Gate Bridge.

20°

DREW

ANDREW "DREW" JOHN LACHEY

BIRTHDATE: August 8, 1976

STAR SIGN: Leo

BIRTHPLACE: Cincinnati, Ohio

HEIGHT: 5' 6"

WEIGHT: 148 lbs.

HAIR: Brown

EYES: Hazel

PARENTS: Cate and John

SIBLINGS: Brother Nick, 25; stepsister Josie, 17; half-brother Isaac, 7; adopted brother Zac, 5; adopted sister Kaitlin, 4; adopted sister Sally, 7; adopted brother Timothy, 6

FAVORITE PERFORMERS: Marvin Gaye, Prince, Take 6

FAVORITE SONG: "Purple Rain" by Prince

FAVORITE FOODS: Pizza, doughnuts, junk food

FAVORITE DRINK: Lemonade

FAVORITE COLOR: Navy blue

FAVORITE SPORTS: Basketball and football

FAVORITE TEAM: Kansas City Chiefs

FAVORITE ACTORS: Mel Gibson, Harrison Ford

FAVORITE ACTRESS: Minnie Driver

FAVORITE MOVIE: *Braveheart*

FAVORITE 98° SONG: "She's Out of My Life"

FAVORITE COLLECTOR'S ITEM: Baseball caps

FAVORITE CHILDHOOD TOY, ACCORDING TO MOM: *Star Wars* action figures

VITAL STATISTICS

"I LIKE A GIRL WHO IS READY TO GO OUT THERE AND LIVE LIFE. I'M ADVENTUROUS AND WILL TRY ANYTHING AT LEAST ONCE—MAYBE TWO OR THREE TIMES."

Although Drew Lachey attended a performing-arts school from the time he was 8 years old, no one was more surprised than he was that he ended up a pop star. "When I got out of high school I immediately joined the Army. I went through basic training and then medic training and became an emergency medical technician. I joined the reserves and moved to Brooklyn, New York," the youngest member of the group says. "I was content living the blue-collar life. I went to work every day and did my job and enjoyed it. I played softball with some of the guys I worked with and had an ordinary life."

Why would a Midwestern boy come so far East? "What better place to break into the whole medical scene and to be an ambulance driver than New York?" he answers. "It's emergency central over there. I thought that I might as well just go there and jump in with both feet."

Drew shared an apartment with his best friend from high

Thinking about what cap to put on?

Nick came and picked me up at the airport. In the car he was talking about the changes going on in the group. We talked about it more that night when Drew was there, and I said, just jokingly, that Drew should join the group. We had gone to see *Miss Saigon* that night, and Drew talked about how seeing that made him realize how much he missed performing. But he had always talked about doing search and rescue, and I thought he was doing what he wanted. I didn't think he would just drop everything and join the group when Nick called him a week later. I thought it was great but it

school in Brooklyn, and when asked how many people he saved, he says, "All I remember is that I lost one. I have no idea how many lives I may have saved. EMTs always remember the ones they lost."

Although Drew loved his job and his new life in New York, he did feel that something was missing. That something was music, which his big brother, Nick, was pursuing out in California. "I was always talking to Nick on the phone and I was always keeping track of what the group was doing," he recalls. "But I missed the singing aspect of my life ever since I graduated high school. I just didn't

want to do the starving-artist thing, and I decided that I'd rather just follow this other passion of mine."

"Drew's joining the group was definitely more of a surprise," his mom, Cate, remembers. "When Drew was living in New York, Nick called me to say that he was going to visit Drew. I had a few days off and I decided to join them in New York and spend a couple days with the two. I flew out, and Drew was at work so

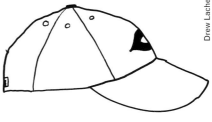

Draw's Hat - 7⅛

was a surprise to me because I thought that Drew was settled in what he was doing." She's quick to add that she's thrilled that

her boys are together. "At least I know that when they are on the other side of the world and have a 104° fever one has got the other with him."

Drew's whole life changed with that fateful phone call from his brother, urging him to join his singing group. "When Nick called

Drew Lachey

"IT WAS LIKE A WHOLE FIRE WAS RELIT. IT JUST FELT RIGHT. I KNEW IT WAS JUST MEANT TO BE."

me up and gave me this opportunity, it was like a whole fire was relit. It just felt right. I knew it was just meant to be."

Drew jumped at the chance to be the band's baritone. "I was actually kind of taken by surprise by the whole thing because I knew that they had made some connections and that they were doing well, and they would get signed pretty soon. With everything going so great I was surprised that they would take a chance on a new guy."

Nick flew to New York, and the two brothers packed up Drew's car and drove across the country. When Drew got to L.A. he, like the other guys, took on odd jobs while waiting for their careers to take off. "I had to work the graveyard shift at Jerry's Deli in L.A.," he says. "It's like this upscale deli, and a lot of celebrities go in there. I worked making shakes and sundaes and pouring soup. Every night when I would go to work the other guys would be just going out to hang out with friends or rent a movie or something. When I would come back from work at 6 in the morning, they would all be asleep. It was just miserable."

But as Drew was waiting tables, success was waiting just

"Oh Snap!!"

around the corner. Performing with his brother Nick and old pal Justin just like the "old days" at The School for Creative and Performing Arts in Cincinnati made paying his dues a lot easier.

His experience at the School for Performing Arts started it all, Drew thinks. He claims his years there cultivated a deep love of music. "The school went from fourth grade to twelfth grade and it was part of the Cincinnati public school system, but you had to audition to get in," he says. "They focused just as much on the arts as they did academics. It was very helpful. Every day when I'm backstage I really appreciate what I learned at that school and what type of effect it had on me."

Though Drew was only 8 when he auditioned to get into the school, he remembers the whole process. "For art you had to draw; for vocal music you had to sing 'My Country 'Tis of Thee'; for drama they gave you a passage to read. For the younger kids it was Dr. Seuss and for the older kids it was something from Shakespeare.

Christmas time.

Courtesy Cate Fompa and Family.

24°

"I was a drama and vocal-music major. We were always doing plays and musicals," he goes on. "I also played drums, and was in choir and a vocal group called Meridian Eight. I think that's where I got my passion for music—in Meridian Eight. The two vocal teachers played a big role in my wanting to become a singer and appreciation for all different types of music. We did a really eclectic mix of music, everything from jazz to salsa to *Carmina Burana*."

Little did he know that one day he'd be riding an express train to superstardom—and enjoying every minute. "It really is a once-in-a-lifetime opportunity," he says. " I mean, we got to go to the Super Bowl, and we got to meet people like Stevie Wonder. Just the other day we met Kevin Costner. He brought his daughter to our show in L.A., and he came backstage after the show. We got to hang out with him and take our picture with him. That was just really cool."

But Drew admits that fame isn't always rosy. "We're not even anywhere close to as famous as some stars are, and already we've started to lose a little bit of privacy," he says. "It's not a big thing, but you take things like privacy for granted when you have them and you want to have them back."

"I miss the ability to be able to come and go as I please," he continues. "And having the flexibility in my schedule to see my family and hang out with my friends. We are always on the road—we've been on the road since the summer of '97. So I really haven't had that many opportunities to see my parents unless they come to a show or at the holidays or something. I think that's what I miss most about the old life before 98°. That and being able to call in sick

to work, or take a long weekend to go see my parents, or hang out with my friends and shoot some pool."

How is he able to keep his ego from exploding, with all of the attention he's

receiving these days? "Being in a group like this helps you stay grounded," he answers. "As a solo artist, you're always surrounded by yes men and people kissing up to you and telling you how good you are. In a group you have other people around you giving you feedback and creative criticism, not just 'Oh, that show was great.' Also, I think my family plays a big part in keeping us humble—especially my dad. He's very proud of us, and I think he realizes how big this is becoming, but he really tries to make everything seem normal. We talk on the phone about the same things —sports, my love life, how my little brother is doing."

"I think both my sons were real centered when they started the

Courtesy Cate Fompa and Family

Drew's got Nick covered.

group," Drew's mother adds. "They still come back and hang out with their old friends. That center core is still really important to them. Even though they are becoming very successful, their core will always stay with people who care about them for who they are, and not just because they are in 98°."

Drew is very close with his family. He's in touch with them several times a week by phone, and he considers them a huge support. In fact, his mother, Cate, is the president of the 98° fan club. "She built an addition on her house for a fan-club office, and had extra phone lines put in," he says proudly. "It's like she works two jobs—her day job and the fan club."

The family support doesn't stop there. "My grandmother wears the 98° button on her sweater all the time," he continues. "She watches MTV now, and MTV is not something you would expect my grandmother to watch. She'll say, 'You were No. 2 on *Total Request*'."

For a while Drew was used to being the youngest son of Cate, a prevention coordinator at a university, and John, a pharmacist. But now he has more siblings than

Making a big splash.

"DREW WAS ALWAYS THE CLOWN, THE ENTERTAINER, THE ONE WHO WOULD ALWAYS MAKE YOU FEEL BETTER. HE WAS SENSITIVE AND FUNNY AT THE SAME TIME."

he ever imagined. He is second oldest to a stepsister, a half-brother, and four adopted siblings.

Drew fondly remembers growing up in the Midwest. "I had a great childhood. I played baseball, I played soccer, did gymnastics," he says. "My parents divorced when I was 3, and I may have come from a broken home but we were never without a father or a mother. My father never lived more than a mile away from us. He always had an active role in our lives and every day he had off during the week he would pick us up after school and we

would have guy time. We spent every weekend together."

"Everyone always supported me and I always had a lot of love in my family," he goes on. "Nick and I were very close when we were growing up, and we've been close our whole lives. We were always really good friends and we were always playing together. When my mom was at work we would play basketball together and entertain each other."

Drew's mother also remembers his growing-up years. "Drew is, and has always been, very much a people person," she recalls.

"Drew as a younger son was always the clown, the entertainer, the one who would always make you feel better. He was sensitive and funny at the same time. He was always a smart aleck, but you knew it was coming out of caring. He would be there to lift spirits and leave little notes, and things like that."

The funniest thing Cate remembers Drew doing as a kid was a killer imitation of Dopey the dwarf. "He would do the hood and get the ears and the talk. It was great!" she says, laughing. "He was always a character.

"Drew was the one who first got into the performing thing because he wanted to do the mime, comedy, and drama part of it," Cate goes on. "He was always very much into people and creating and he wasn't organized at all!"

In his senior year of high school, however, that changed. "He began working as a counselor at a camp," his mom says. "And he was the youngest senior counselor they ever had. That summer he really changed and became amazingly organized and structured. He became the one that always had the calendar and the log and the notes. That has continued into the group, where he is the administrator."

The guys in the group agree.

"He always takes care of the business end of things, and he's very dedicated and passionate," his brother Nick says. "But he's also a smart aleck."

"Definitely sarcastic," Justin agrees. Jeff adds, "But very organized, very polite, very professional."

Drew

Larger than life on the promo bus.

"The guys do look to me as sort of the organized one," Drew agrees. I like to make sure everything runs smoothly."

Professional Drew definitely takes the time to relax, however. Although he wishes he had more spare time, when he isn't working Drew loves sports. "I'm a huge

basketball and football fan, and I just went bowling for the first time in three years. I had a great time. I also like going to the movies, doing regular stuff." He hasn't banged on his old drum set in a while, but Drew is handy with rhythm and in his spare moments he also enjoys songwriting.

But the first thing Drew likes to do in his free time is spend time with the people who are important to him. "I'm seeing someone right now, but we'll just have to wait and see what happens. The traveling makes it difficult."

"HE'S VERY DEDICATED AND PASSIONATE, BUT HE'S ALSO A SMART ALECK."

Drew is the first to admit that his newfound fame makes it easier to meet girls, however. "It is very easy," he says. "Girls like to approach me now and I am constantly around them because I am in a group. It's difficult, though, because I don't know what their motives are. I don't know if they want to get to know me because they like me or because they think I have lots of money or something. You really have to question their motivation—not distrust— but just be a little skeptical of people, which is kind of jaded but it really is true. It is easy to meet girls, but it is hard to build any kind of relationship from the ground up, I think."

Just what does he look for in a girl? "I like a girl who has a good sense of humor and who is down-to-earth," he confides. "I also like someone who likes to have a good time and try new things—a girl who is ready to go out there and live life. I'm adventurous and will try anything at least once—maybe two or three times. I also like someone who is confident, and independent, who could stand on her own without me."

His idea of a great date is "something unplanned. If it's going to be great it will be great on its own and if you try to make it too great it's going to come off cliché and ordinary," he asserts.

It doesn't seem that any date with Drew would be ordinary, and once he commits he throws himself headfirst into a relationship. "Once I drove twenty-four hours straight to surprise a girl I liked," he admits.

When he's not on the road or visiting with family, Drew escapes to his one-bedroom apartment in New York. "It's decorated with pictures of my family, the group—

us with Russell Simmons and Stevie Wonder. I don't have room in my apartment for much. It's just a little place for me to put my stuff and hang out."

He has made room for his baseball cap collection, however, which at last count is more than 100 strong, and mementos from the road. "I like to keep things like a ticket stub from the Bulls' finals

On stage in Toronto.

Johnny Camisa

game or a program from the *Mulan* premiere—anything like that. When I'm 75, I can say I was there. Those are once-in-a-lifetime opportunities that I treasure."

It's apparent that Drew is the sentimental type, especially when it comes to his family. In fact, his grandfather is his personal role model. "He's had health problems, and he was in World War II and Korea," Drew says. "A lot of

MOST EMBARRASSING MOMENTS

ONSTAGE:

"I don't get embarrassed very easily, so you know it's pretty bad when I do. The last time something embarrassing happened onstage, nobody saw it but me, thankfully. I came on from my costume change with my fly all the way down, and I felt a breeze. I was thinking, "Is my fly down?' But I was standing in front of thousands of people and I couldn't check, so I had to wait until a break in the song. It sure was down."

OFFSTAGE:

I was 6 years old and had just learned how to ride a bike, and my dad took my brother and me to this park in Cincinnati. There is this hill and at the bottom you can turn to the right or go into the lake. I just got my bike that day, and I hadn't mastered the art of braking yet, so I went down this hill and I started to turn right. But there were these people standing there and I couldn't get around them, so boom! I went right into the lake. Some guy working at the boat dock jumped into the lake and rescued me. My bike unfortunately was never the same after that."

29°

stuff happened in his life and he has always put his family first. He's fought through strokes and heart attacks and he always keeps his good humor. He is just the sweetest man on the face of the earth, and when I become 75 I want to be like him. I want to have a family that I love and who

are passionate about it, and you work hard, it can happen. There is also a lot of chance and coincidence. You just have to be at the right place at the right time and just really give it all you've got."

Drew's favorite 98° song is their unique a cappella rendition

with an a cappella song like that. If you don't have what it takes, it's going to show up real loud and clear in the harmonies!"

With talent like that, it seems that 98° will have a long, hot career. Drew sure hopes so, but what's more important to him is having a family one day. "Ten

"TEN YEARS FROM NOW, I WANT A FAMILY, AND THE HOUSE WITH THE WHITE PICKET FENCE, AND THE DOG. I WANT THE ALL-AMERICAN DREAM."

respects me. Everything he has now is what I want."

Drew's professional role model is Stevie Wonder, with whom he immensely enjoyed working. He admires Stevie because "he has had such longevity in a business that has such short careers. And he was just so cool to us. He didn't have to do a lot of the stuff he did for us but he went out of his way to help our careers."

Other artists Drew would like to work with include his idols Boyz II Men, or the Gypsy Kings. "Their sound is totally unique and I think it would be cool to break down the barriers of the genres of music," he says.

To aspiring singers, Drew advises, "Stick with it, stay focused and dedicated. If you

of the Michael Jackson hit, "She's Out of My Life," which was arranged by the Lacheys' childhood buddy, Devon Biere. "I think it's a beautiful arrangement. It's just emotions, not track. It's us putting our hearts into the song."

His mom agrees. "Devon is almost like another kid to me, so I feel that link, that the people who were important to them growing up are still important people in their lives. And I just love the fact that the song really shows their talent."

Drew's baritone is a stand out in the piece. "It really shows how the group can sing," Cate continues. "And that they are not just four cute guys who can stand up on a stage. They are four excellent musicians, and you can't fake that

In Hawaii going jet skiing.

years from now, I want a family, and the house with the white picket fence, and the dog. I want the all-American dream," he says.

"Hopefully I'll still be in the music business, though," he adds. "Maybe writing songs, or advising people as a consultant. This business has become such a big part of my life I really can't picture myself getting away from it anytime soon."

JUSTIN

Justin

31°

Courtesy THE WALT DISNEY COMPANY

JUSTIN PAUL JEFFRE

BIRTHDATE: February 25, 1973

STAR SIGN: Pisces

BIRTHPLACE: Mount Clemens, Michigan

HEIGHT: 5' 10"

WEIGHT: 150 lbs.

HAIR: Brown

EYES: Blue

PARENTS: Susan and Dan

SIBLINGS: Brother Dan, 30; half-sister Alexandra, 13

FAVORITE PERFORMERS: James Brown, Stevie Wonder

FAVORITE SONG: "Try A Little Tenderness" by Otis Redding

FAVORITE FOODS: Pizza, doughnuts, Skyline Chili

FAVORITE DRINK: Orange juice

FAVORITE COLOR: Blue

FAVORITE SPORTS: Soccer, tennis

FAVORITE TEAM: Cincinnati Bengals

FAVORITE ACTORS: Robert De Niro

FAVORITE ACTRESS: Jennifer Lopez

FAVORITE MOVIE: *Friday, Braveheart*

FAVORITE 98° SONG: "True to Your Heart"

FAVORITE COLLECTOR'S ITEM: sunglasses

FAVORITE CHILDHOOD TOY, ACCORDING TO MOM: a teddy bear

VITAL STATISTICS

JUSTIN'S DREAM GIRL: "...SOMEBODY WHO HAS A GREAT SENSE OF HUMOR, AND WHO HAS HER OWN THING GOING ON. I DON'T WANT SOMEONE WHO IS LIVING THROUGH MY EXPERIENCES."

"We truly love music," says Justin Jeffre. "Even if we weren't as successful, and still struggling, we would do it anyway. We love to sing and love to be in the studio. Most important, we love to do performances and have people come to the shows who are enthused about what we're doing."

Justin's love of music was apparent from a young age, according to his mother, Susan. "His cousin, Stella, was a student in Performing Arts. They were allowed to bring a friend and he spent the day with her there, and liked it. He auditioned when he was only 11 years old."

Justin remembers the audition like it was yesterday. "I remember I went to audition for drama and I had to be a hot-air balloon. I just puffed my cheeks out and stuck my arms out. I was actually pretty good!" he boasts. "Drama was my major the first year, but later I became a music major. As I got older I only had enough time for a certain amount of classes, so I

Young Justin.

Courtesy Jeffre Family

came from a family that absolutely loved music. He grew up with a lot of singing and dancing. As far as his voice, though, it was as much as a surprise to him as it was to anybody."

But Justin couldn't have been too surprised. He claims that he knew deep inside that pop stardom was his future. "At a very early age I had this dream, but it was more than just a dream," he explains. "It was odd in the sense that I felt like it was something that was going to happen or was meant to happen, not because I thought I was the world's greatest singer or anything. It was a gut feeling. From

dinner, and my father had big-band music on. My father always wore a hat, and Justin always loved hats. There was also a cane hanging on the coat rack. We had just finished eating, and we were all sitting around the dining room table, with the music playing in the background. Justin came out and did a little soft-shoe, with his grandfather's hat and the cane. I just looked at him and said 'Well, thank you, Justin.' He was only about 11 or 12."

At Performing Arts, Justin honed his vocal and stage skills. He learned the trombone, and made a friend for life in Nick

concentrated on music.

"When I went to sign the papers, the secretary said that he must be really talented

"AT A VERY EARLY AGE I HAD THIS DREAM. IT WAS ODD IN THE SENSE THAT I FELT LIKE IT WAS SOMETHING THAT WAS GOING TO HAPPEN OR WAS MEANT TO HAPPEN... I ALWAYS BELIEVED THAT IF YOU REALLY WANTED SOMETHING AND YOU WORKED HARD TOWARD IT, YOU COULD REALIZE IT."

because they had auditioned a hundred kids, and only chose ten, including him," Justin's mother says. Justin was only in the sixth grade, and before that his mom had no idea about her son's talent. "I wasn't even sure that I was happy that he was making a change, from the private school he was in, to public school," she admits. "But he

the seventh grade I used to pray about it. I always believed that if you really wanted something and you worked hard toward it, you could realize it."

Justin's mother says that as a child, young Justin was full of antics. "One of my favorite memories is from after he joined Performing Arts. We were having Thanksgiving

Lachey. "I started singing with Nick there," he recalls. "At the time there was this new group out called Take 6. They were an a cappella group, and the teachers brought them to our attention. They played the album for us in class. I went out to get the album myself, and I was just blown away by it. It really inspired me."

"One day I was walking through the halls and I heard people singing Take 6, and it was Nick and some other guys," he goes on. "They were practicing for this concert the school was putting on that was a tribute to Dr. Martin Luther King. I walked in and knew I wanted to be a part of it, because of these guys who were singing Take 6 and also because I am a great admirer of Dr. King. So I became involved in that show with Nick and from then on we enjoyed singing that type of music together, with all the harmonies. We would come in before school and sing and stay after school and sing."

Justin's booming bass proved to be the perfect counterpoint to Nick's tenor. "After that, we always sang together. We got into a barbershop quartet, and worked in an amusement park. Later I was with an R&B band, singing doo-wop and soul. I got Nick to come and join that group, too."

Later on, Nick would return the favor by inviting Justin to join the band that would become 98°. "A few weeks after Nick moved out to L.A. he called me and said, 'You got to come out here. We've got a lot going on!' It didn't take more than a second to convince me. We had always talked about going out to L.A. and pursuing

our dreams. As soon as Nick called, I knew the timing was right."

But before Justin packed his things and jumped on the next plane, he had to break the news to his mom, which he knew wasn't going to be easy. "I knew that it was brewing and he called and told me he was moving to California," his mother recalls. "And I said, 'Just like that?' I spent the day crying. When I came home from work, he was there and I was teary-eyed. He asked me how long I was going to be crying and I said, 'I don't know.' He said that didn't make him feel good."

But she soon got over it, and she became Justin's biggest supporter. "My family has been great and they have always been supportive from the very beginning," Justin says of his mom, who works in the accounting division of an airline. His father is a computer consultant.

Justin stays in touch with his mom at least once a week, and he says she has always championed his singing. "There have been times when Nick and I have been in between groups, and there were times when I had some bad experiences and I didn't want to be in a group right then. My mom was like, 'You guys should be out there and you know you've got the talent.' She was definitely sup-

portive, and she always encouraged me."

"There was no doubt in my mind that these guys were going to be a great success," Susan asserts. "I believe that they have extraordinary talent. For me it was the natural progression. Things happen because you make them happen. You set your goals and

Early musical talent.

you don't stop until you get there. And that combination, with extraordinary talent, is what did it for Justin. There was never any doubt in my mind that it would."

Susan is a huge fan of Justin's work, and her favorite 98° song is "Take My Breath Away" from their debut album. "It's one of the most beautiful songs I've ever heard,"

Courtesy Jeffre Family

"A nation that expects to be ignorant and free, wants what never was and never will be." Thomas Jefferson

she says. "When I heard just the introduction I said, that's the one I've been waiting for.'"

Justin was a "doll baby," his mother recalls. "I used to call him 'angel pie.' He was a little stubborn, but I could always get around it." As a toddler, Justin's favorite toy was a stuffed bear. "The first time his father and I took him in a department store, he was too young to know that you don't pick a toy up and put it under your arm." But he did, and it was soon his. In fact, it is still his. "When we took stuff to Goodwill, I couldn't get rid of the bear, and he couldn't do it, so he came back home with the stuffed animal," she remembers, laughing.

Justin says his childhood was "normal." He grew up with an older brother, Dan, a computer programmer who is now 30. "We never had a lot of money and went through tough times in that sense, but we had a strong family and that made it OK. We made it through just fine and I am probably stronger

for it now. I never missed out on anything, in spite of being somewhat poor. There were a lot of great experiences, and I feel very fortunate to have had the childhood that I had."

After Performing Arts school, Justin enrolled in the University of Cincinnati to study history and political science. But though he was exploring other interests, he didn't give up his passion for music. "I played in a band that performed in a lot of redneck bars around Ohio. Every weekend we had a gig—it was a nice weekend job and a good experience. I think it helped me grow as a performer and musician. Otherwise, I had a pretty normal life. I spent a lot of time hanging out with my friends."

Justin's mom doesn't think that her son has changed at all with the success of 98°. "The real Justin shines through. He is pretty much how you see him onstage or in an interview. He has a lot of depth, and he has an ability to sift through the extraneous and see the bottom

line. He's very good-natured."

How does Justin manage to keep his feet on the ground with his newfound fame? "I think we are all pretty down-to-earth to begin with," he confides. "It was a little bit of a rocky road after our first single, and that sort of taught us early on that as quickly as you rise up, you can be gone. It taught us that we had to keep working hard no matter what and never forget where we came from. We're really not different. We're just more fortunate."

Justin's mother has her own theory. "When he started Performing Arts he was immediately so involved," she recalls. "He just threw himself into that school. He starred in Oliver, and he ate, drank, and slept it. He knew everyone's part. The routine that he has now is similar to back then. He's been living at this pace since he was at Performing Arts and I think that's why he hasn't changed much. He's used to the pace, and he's always had much going on."

It was also Justin's appreciation for hard work that made him a success, Susan thinks. While growing up Justin had to do his share of grunt work, like washing dishes. "Someone in my family worked in a restaurant and convinced me to take a job there," he recalls. "It was really far away, so by the time I bought gas and then food, because I would be hungry after work at the end of the day, I hardly made any money. And it was really hard work."

While Justin doesn't miss that part of life pre-98°, he does sometimes wish he had the free time he did back then. "Sometimes, the job never stops," he points out.

Justin at 21 with Cujo.

Courtesy Jeffre Family

"Sometimes you can't really just relax and do the same thing you would normally do."

And there is the privacy issue, too. "When you're having a meal people sometimes just don't think about that as my only time in a day to sit down and just have a nice quiet meal with somebody. They think about getting an autograph. It's a downside, but it's not too much of a sacrifice to make us want to stop what we're doing."

Justin feels it's a pretty fair trade-off for the upside to fame. "The best thing for me is getting

"AS QUICKLY AS YOU RISE UP YOU CAN BE GONE...WE'RE REALLY NOT DIFFERENT. WE'RE JUST MORE FORTUNATE."

Justin Jeffre

to meet famous people who I've always looked up to, like Stevie Wonder, or Boyz II Men," he says. "We also got to meet Jennifer Lopez recently. It's great to go somewhere and meet people you've wanted to meet since you were a little kid. We meet all different types of people everywhere we go."

Fame does take its toll on his love life, however. "I don't really have a girlfriend but there is one girl that I am interested in. It's really not the right time now. Life on the road is very difficult, and it is hard to maintain a relationship.

Some days you don't even have time to pick up the phone and talk to them before they would be asleep. And then there's the trust factor," he adds. "We meet girls all the time, and it's not like we're the world's coolest guys, but sometimes these girls just throw themselves at us. Even if you are not the type of guy—which none of us really are—who will go out there and get all the girls you can, I think people sort of think that's how we should act, or that's what they would do. They expect you to act a certain way. It makes it difficult when you are in a relationship. You have to

Johnny Camisa

Sound check, Toronto.

Justin has a deep romantic streak, and once he even wrote a song for a girl who caught his eye. "I didn't consider myself a song-writer at the time," he admits. "And I just went ahead and wrote a song for her. She was flattered, so I guess it worked in that sense. I didn't end up getting the girl, so I guess it really didn't work."

Don't be fooled by Justin's mellow exterior. Though he describes himself as "the most levelheaded" guy in the group, the others say that he is a renowned party lover. But Justin insists that no matter what, he likes to stay cool, calm, and collected. "There are a lot of things that can be pretty dramatic on the road. There are things that you just can't let get you too upset. Sometimes if you can keep a cool head and find a solution, it will go a little faster than when people get all riled up and let their emotions get to them. It's better not to make decisions in the heat of the moment that might not be the best and you might regret in the future."

"IT'S BETTER NOT TO MAKE DECISIONS IN THE HEAT OF THE MOMENT THAT MIGHT NOT BE THE BEST AND YOU MIGHT REGRET IN THE FUTURE."

trust her, she has to trust you. And you have to deal with the fact that you are rarely going to see her, maybe every other month if you're lucky. It's really difficult. I've sort of accepted the fact that it will probably be a little while before I can have a serious relationship."

When he does commit, Justin says it will be to "somebody who has a great sense of humor, and who has her own thing going on. I don't want someone who is living through my experiences. I want

someone who has her own interests and her own goals."

This lucky girl can expect a date that would include "romantic dinners and beautiful natural settings, like a park or a beach." Justin is quick to add, "As long as you are with the right person, a good time could be something as simple as going bowling, or going to a movie, or shooting pool. Just getting to know the other person and enjoying each other's company—that's a great date."

Drew, Nick, and Jeff say that Justin's view of himself is dead-on. "Justin is compassionate, charis-matic, and no one dislikes him," Jeff says.

"He definitely has a cool, even head," Nick agrees.

But Drew points out the lurking wild man underneath the surface. He's laid-back, cool, but he's a partyer," he says.

Justin enjoys partying with his pals in the band the most, and he never misses an opportunity to have fun with his old friends, too. "When I go back home to Ohio, I like to hang out with my friends, shoot pool, and check out local bands," he says. "I also love to play video games, and whenever we get the chance we like to go out to the new arcades and play the virtual-reality kind of stuff. I really get into that stuff."

Home to Justin still is Cincinnati, though he says he's hardly ever there and that he's been on the road so much that he hasn't had the time to find his own digs yet. "Whenever I get the chance I go to Cincinnati. That's where all my friends and family are. It's comfortable and familiar there," he says.

Justin has two role models that he looks to for guidance in his personal and professional lives. "I had a great vocal teacher who was really cool," he says. "She would be your friend, but if you were goofing off in class she would straighten you up. Also, Stevie Wonder is a role model. He sings music about issues, about racism and classism. And in his personal life he comes off as a very strong yet caring person. He gets involved with a lot of causes and charities. For instance, he was a major part of bringing about the Martin Luther King holiday. I really admire him for that as well as people who are like that."

Speaking of Stevie Wonder, guess what Justin's favorite 98° song is? "'True to Your Heart,'" he answers. "Because we got to work with Stevie. It was such a great honor, and even if our records weren't doing well, I would still be incredibly proud of the whole thing. That's something that no one can ever take away from us."

98° kicks back in Florida.

38°

Justin

Promo bus shot.

Johnny Camisa

like to work with Take 6, because I am such a big fan. I think they are the masters of a cappella singing. And Quincy Jones. He has worked with everybody I have ever idolized, from Ella Fitzgerald to all the great jazz artists in the past to the new hip-hop artists. He can bring something out of every type of artist, and we were fortunate enough to meet him once. I think Babyface is great, too, and the Artist—I think he is one of the most talented musicians around."

In ten years, Justin says, you will still find him making music. "I want will keep him around as a musician for many years to come. To aspiring singers, he offers this piece of advice: "Work hard, and believe in yourself even when people tell you you'll never make it, because we had people tell us that, too." He quickly adds, remembering the group's breakthrough discovery, "And sing for anyone who will listen. You never know who is going to give you a break. But do it for the right reasons. Do it because you love to sing, not because it's going to make you a millionaire. If you do that you are in for a long, tough ride."

"IN TEN YEARS... I WANT TO BE PERFORMING BUT IT DOESN'T HAVE TO BE ON THE SCALE THAT IT IS NOW. I COULD SEE MYSELF IN A SMALL BAR JUST SINGING SOME TYPE OF JAZZ STANDARD."

Justin says he would jump at the chance to work with Stevie Wonder again, and there are others whose sound he feels would blend perfectly with 98°. "Musically, Lenny Kravitz would be a great mix," he points out. "With his type of harmony, his edge with our edge would be something unique. I would also

to be performing but it doesn't have to be on the scale that it is now," he says. "I could see myself in a small bar just singing some type of jazz standard. I would enjoy that as much as I do this... well... probably not as much. I would definitely enjoy that, and I would love to do other things. There was a time when I almost joined a salsa band. I would just like to keep growing as a musician."

Justin's talent and dedication

Celebrating at the Platinum Party.

Julie Blattberg

Julie Blattberg

MOST EMBARRASSING MOMENTS

ONSTAGE:

"One time I split my pants while I was dancing. I just kept on going, and laughed about it."

OFFSTAGE:

"One time I sent this girl some flowers. She was a good friend, and I liked her for a long time, so I sent her some flowers. We were over at her place and she and her two sisters were trying to decide what to get their mom for her birthday. Somebody said, 'Flowers,' but the girl I liked said, 'No, that's a stupid gift. Why would you get someone something that's already dead?' Needless to say I was pretty embarrassed."

NICK

Courtesy THE WALT DISNEY COMPANY.

NICHOLAS "NICK" SCOTT LACHEY

BIRTHDATE: November 9, 1973

STAR SIGN: Scorpio

BIRTHPLACE: Harlan, Kentucky

HEIGHT: 5' 10"

WEIGHT: 180 lbs.

HAIR: Brown

EYES: Blue

PARENTS: Cate and John

SIBLINGS: Brother Drew, 23; stepsister Josie, 17; half-brother Isaac, 7; adopted brother Zac, 5; adopted sister Kaitlin, 4; adopted sister Sally, 7; adopted brother Timothy, 6

FAVORITE PERFORMERS: Boyz II Men, Sade, Jodeci, Brian McKnight, Take 6

FAVORITE SONG: "Cherish the Day" by Sade

FAVORITE FOODS: Skyline Chili, steak, pizza, barbecue

FAVORITE DRINK: Yoo-Hoo

FAVORITE COLOR: Red

FAVORITE SPORTS: Football, basketball

FAVORITE TEAMS: Cincinnati Bengals, Cincinnati Reds

FAVORITE ACTOR: Bruce Willis

FAVORITE ACTRESS: Michelle Pfeiffer

FAVORITE MOVIE: *Die Hard*

FAVORITE 98° SONG: "Heaven's Missing an Angel"

FAVORITE COLLECTOR'S ITEM: CDs

FAVORITE CHILDHOOD TOY, ACCORDING TO MOM: Richard Scarry's *Puzzle Town*

VITAL STATISTICS

"MY IDEAL GIRL IS A CONFIDENT INDIVIDUAL, BEAUTIFUL INSIDE AND OUTSIDE, WHO LIKES TO HAVE A GOOD TIME."

Believe it or not, Nick Lachey credits sibling rivalry with igniting his interest in show business. "I was 12, in seventh grade, when Drew auditioned for the School for Performing Arts. He auditioned because he was such a ham," the lead tenor says. "He got in and my family made such a huge deal about it and about how talented he was. So I decided that I was going to go down there and audition too, and show these people that it wasn't such a big deal. So I did and I got in. I ended up going and fell in love with it and never left. It's funny because originally I didn't want to go."

Nick sailed right through his audition. "For drama, I had to act like I was sneaking up on someone and scare them. For vocal music, I sang 'My Country 'Tis of Thee.' I had to draw something for art, and I had to write a story for creative writing."

Nick and Drew's mother, Cate, remembers that time well: "We were living in a school district where I really didn't want Nick going into the junior high. So we were looking at moving, and we were looking at schools in Cincinnati and I noticed they had the performing-arts school. Drew showed interest

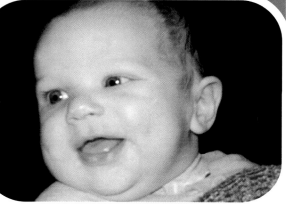

Breaking hearts from the start.

in it. The school district also had a college prep school, so I thought we would audition Drew, and Nick could go to the college prep school," she reminisces.

"So we went down and Drew had his audition. After Drew's audition, Nick said that he wanted to audition too. Nick just wanted to show that he could get in. He really didn't talk about going there. He just talked about auditioning. But when his scores came back, I knew I was going to have them both going to the School for Performing Arts."

But Nick claims his relationship

with little brother Drew no longer thrives on competition. "It has changed," Nick says. "It's very different from what it was. We have always been close, but as little kids we had that typical

Nick with baby brother Drew.

brotherly rivalry. We would always compete, and we would get into fights a lot. Drew would start stuff and I would kill him— typical things."

"In high school, all the teachers would have me in their classrooms, then have him," Nick continues, "And I think it was tough on him to play second fiddle. As we become older, after high school, I had my set of friends, and he had his set of friends.

Then when I went to college, I think we both grew up a lot and became more friends than brothers. That is the point where all the pettiness was gone. Drew started to get his own identity and then

"NICK... WAS ALWAYS THE RESPONSIBLE ONE GROWING UP. . . NICK WAS ALWAYS THERE. YOU COULD ALWAYS COUNT ON HIM."

Nick in 1974.

Courtesy Cate Fompa and Family

he went to the Army and matured a lot there. For the past five years, we've been more best friends than anything else."

While Nick's mom was surprised about Drew's decision to follow in his big brother's footsteps, she wasn't the least bit fazed about Nick's quick exit to L.A. "I told him to go for it," Cate says. "He was always talking about moving out there, and when the opportunity came he said, 'Mom what should I do? I'm in school.' I told him, 'You'll always wonder if you don't go. Even if it doesn't work, it's better than to always wonder. College will always be there.' This was an opportunity he had to grab then. He couldn't have gotten this chance the same way again."

"I got a call Memorial Day weekend 1995 from Jon, a friend of mine that I went to high school with," Nick remembers. "He said he met this guy in L.A., who turned out to be Jeff. I was still in Cincinnati at the time and they were trying to put this music thing together out in L.A., and they needed one more guy. He wanted to know if I would be interested in coming out there."

Nick was initially skeptical. "When I first heard about it, I didn't trust him on it. I didn't know this guy, Jeff, but then I talked to him on the phone, and I heard him sing over the phone, and he heard me sing. The more I heard from him, the more convinced I became that this was the right thing to do. It was a time in my life when I think

Courtesy Cate Fompa and Family

Nick at age 10.

I was ready for a change, so it just kind of worked."

Nick admits he was a bit torn about leaving school. "I was a sports medicine major at Miami University in Ohio, and I enjoyed school, but at the same time I wasn't really motivated. The two loves of my life were music and sports," Nick says.

He remembers singing with pal Justin Jeffre as the highlight of that time in his life. "At the same time I was in college, I was singing with Justin in an R&B band called The Avenues. I really enjoyed doing that. I didn't really make any money; it was a weekend thing, but I enjoyed doing it. I had more fun doing that than studying

or anything else, and I could really feel the energy that I got from singing. So when I got the call from L.A., I was definitely ready for a change. I was at a point where I wasn't fully enjoying college."

That wouldn't be the first change Nick would make in his education. It seemed he just couldn't find his niche in any school. "My first year, I went to the University of Southern California," Nick explains. "Initially when I got out of high school, I wanted to be an actor, and I started going into that. As I went on I left the singing behind me and got more into sports, until Justin called me one day and asked me to sing in the R&B band with him."

Nick made the right choice

44°

both times. The first decision reconnected him with his childhood buddy, Justin, who would soon become a crucial member

On tour in the Philippines.

of the group coming together in Los Angeles. Meeting Jeff Timmons formed the core of the artists soon to be known as 98°.

When Drew joined the group, Nick found it great to have a familiar face with him on his road to superstardom. "Family is so important to me," Nick confides. "My parents divorced when I was in the first grade, but that didn't matter. I have a real loving family, and even after the divorce my dad never lived more than five minutes away from me. He was always there for Drew and me, and we were always well loved and well taken care of. We grew up in a pretty typical Midwest situation."

Nick's mom remembers her son growing up: "Nick was—and is—a terrific son. He was always the responsible one growing up. I was a single mother for a long time when I was raising them, and he was always the one who would want to help around the house, and when things needed to be fixed, always the one that tried to step in," she says. "That was always a debate between us. I appreciated the help on one hand, but on the other hand it was like, 'Nick, you are still a kid and it is not your job to be the man of the house.' So there was always that balance that we tried to maintain—me taking his help but not abusing it, and letting him still be a kid. When I was remarried, which was during his senior year in high school, it finally gave him a chance to relax and do the kid thing. I was really glad about it; he just relaxed and let loose a little bit. But he has always been very responsible and an incredible perfectionist, and that still continues."

Did she say responsible? Nick will tell you otherwise when he thinks of some of the teenage antics he pulled. "When I was in high school I used to sneak out of my house, steal my mom's car, and drive to my girlfriend's house to see her in the middle of the night,"

he says. "One time I actually fell asleep at my girlfriend's house. My mom woke up in the morning, and when she saw that her car wasn't there, she panicked. I think I was grounded for the whole rest of high school. You do stupid things when you're young and you're in love, and you think that the world is going to end if you don't get there that night."

"Well, he wasn't perfect," Cate quickly adds. "I am not going to say that, but both my sons were terrific, and Nick was always there.

Double trouble.

Nick

45°

You could always count on him."

If Drew was the family ham, when exactly did she notice her older son's talent? "I remember Nick singing as far back as 5 or 6 years old, but probably when we knew he really had a great voice was at his sixth-grade graduation, when he was doing some solo stuff," Cate says. "When he was in ninth grade, he did *A Christmas Carol*, and there was no music to it—it was pure acting. He was incredible and he won a principal's award for that."

But the time he really blew everyone away was during a performance of Bernstein's "Mass." "That was when he was a junior in high school," Cate continues. "Bernstein's daughter was there for that, it was kind of a tribute to him, and she was just amazed. People walked out of there and walked up to me and said, 'We still have goose bumps all over us.' He won another principal's award for that one, too."

"When he was 14, he was in the show *Little Mary Sunshine*," his mom goes on. "He played the part of the bumbling author who fell in love for the first time, and it was an 'Aw, shucks' kind of role, which was real different from the kind of things he had done. That let his comic side come through.

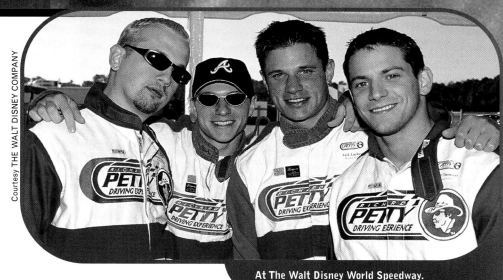

At The Walt Disney World Speedway.

So there were different stages of development to his talent, where I noticed different pieces of it at different times."

The first song she remembers her son singing was "You Are My Sunshine." "It was a family song," Cate explains. "I also remember Nick singing the Whitney Houston song "The Greatest Love of All." He sang that in the sixth-grade. That was the first real serious solo that he did."

When Nick wasn't singing or acting, he was either enjoying sports like soccer or football, wailing on the saxophone, or playing quietly with his brother. "When he was real young, Nick was really into Richard Scarry stuff," his mother recalls. "He liked to play with Puzzle Town, where you could build the buildings and play with people and little plastic cars. We still have it and our kids love it

now. Mayor Fox was Nick's favorite and the police officer was Drew's favorite. They were also into a lot of *Star Wars* stuff."

Nick says he had a "pretty typical Midwestern" childhood, and his family was always there for him when he needed them. "Both my parents have always supported me," he says. "My mom's always been the more spontaneous one, and my dad the rational one, but both have been supportive of everything I've done. They always did their best to make anything happen for me."

"When the opportunity came to join this group, my mom said, 'Go for it,' and my dad did too," Nick reflects. "They said, 'You can always go back to school,' so they made me feel a lot better about my decision. They both are enjoying the

46°

47°

Julie Blattberg

success that we're having. I think it's more fun for them than it is for us!" he jokes.

Not that Nick isn't having fun. Fame does have its perks. "I get to meet a lot of people, like sports idols," he says, "And that's the biggest thing for me—to meet my sports heroes. I can also get into clubs a lot more easily. There are definitely lots of advantages. It's a strange experience being a celebrity, though. There are a lot of different things happening at once."

But there are things Nick misses about the simple life. "I miss being a nobody sometimes," he says. "I miss the privacy, and just the opportunity to sit around and watch a game on Sunday. We're so busy that a lot of the time we don't have the chance to do the things we want to do. But I'm sure it's like that with a lot of professions. Everyone's got a job and things they need to take care of. The loss of privacy is probably a small price to pay in the end."

One thing he doesn't miss about being a nobody is some of the awful jobs he had, like cutting grass. "One summer I cut grass using like a forty-inch industrial mower," he reluctantly remembers. "I probably walked eight miles every day. It was like ninety-eight degrees out— a little pun there. It was a really

miserable job for no money at all."

Remembering experiences like that helps Nick maintain perspective. "It's easy for me to stay grounded and humble," he says. "I think by nature, we're all grounded. We come from solid backgrounds, and growing up in the Midwest is as far from Hollywood as you can be. I think it really helps if you have a foundation to come from. Being on the road with my brother, and my best friends—we all kind of check each other in. When one of us is out of line, we let each other know. We never want to be looked at as a cocky group and get ahead of ourselves. We never wanted that."

If keeping his feet on the ground isn't the hardest part of being famous, then what is? "Having a relationship," he says, without hesitation. "That is one of the hardest things about being famous. When I started the group I had an eight-year relationship, and it took a toll on us. I mean, you're just not there to give her the time she deserves. It's hard. You're not always together and available to each other. But I think if you are dedicated enough you can make it work."

"I don't have any specific type of girl," Nick goes on. "But I think my ideal girl is confident in herself, has her own thing going on. A lot

ONSTAGE:

"Before we got signed we did this show in Dallas. It was the National Cheerleading Association convention, and I was doing a song with these tight overalls on, and one of the straps snapped. I thought I was OK because I was still covered, but then I made a move, and the other one popped off. The pants fell straight down to the floor. I had the mike in one had, and I grabbed my pants with the other just before they went below my waistline and pulled them back up real fast. So I was singing and holding them up at the same time. It was embarrassing not only because of the cheerleaders— there were a lot of parents and grand- parents there and a lot of them thought it was a choreographed move, so I caught a little heat from them after! Another time I tried to jump on a chair onstage and landed flat on my back. You have to just play those things off and have fun with them. If you can't laugh at yourself, you're in big trouble."

OFFSTAGE:

"I think it was the time I stole my mom's car to see my girlfriend. As soon as I got back I was like, 'Mom, please don't call Dad.' She said, 'I already have,' and I remember walking over to his house and sitting on the couch and he did not say a word to me. I was embarrassed about the whole thing, and the fact that it hurt the both of them so much."

48°

"I GUESS I AM INTENSE ONLY BECAUSE I CARE. . . EVERYTHING IN MY LIFE I APPROACH WITH A REAL INTENSE ATTITUDE. IT CAN BE GOOD AND BAD; I TRY TO BALANCE IT OUT."

of times when you're in a group you meet someone and your world becomes her world. I think it's important that your girlfriend have her own stuff going on and her own dreams and goals. I think that my ideal is a confident individual, beautiful inside and outside, who likes to have a good time. I'm a pretty easygoing person, and there are times in my life when I don't like to be brought down, so she should be upbeat."

Nick's idea of a great date? "A great date can only happen when you reach that comfort with some-body," he says thoughtfully. "I think that dating is fun in the early stages when you are finding out about each other, and there is a little discomfort there. But I think that the really great date happens when you are completely comfortable with that person, and you are experiencing things together, and don't have to worry about 'Is my hair out of place?' or 'Is this wrong, is that wrong?' and you just have fun. It's a fun thing just to enjoy each other."

Offstage, when he's not dating or visiting with his family, Nick likes "anything having to do with

sports, going to the movies, or hanging out in clubs, or chowing down on Skyline Chili."

Skyline Chili? It's a restaurant chain in Ohio, and they also sell it in a can, or frozen. "It's not like normal chili with baked beans in it," Nick explains. "We used to eat it over spaghetti, or over a hot dog. Every time we go home it's the first place we go. I actually crave it when I'm not there. Supposedly there's a secret ingredient. I think it's brown sugar."

Home these days for Nick is Cincinnati, though like his brother Drew, he did give the Big Apple a shot. "I tried the New York thing, and I felt myself losing my mind," he says. "I just don't do well in New York. It's too much stress for me and I don't know how to let it roll off. Whenever I have a spare minute, I go back to Cincinnati."

In fact, Nick finds it impractical to have a place to call his own right now. "People may not under-stand or believe it, but in the last two years, I've had maybe one month off," he points out. "It would be nice to have an apartment, but I would never see it and that would frustrate me. I stay with my dad

when I go home."

While on the road, Nick tries to keep a steady workout routine, as is evident from his incredibly buff bod. "I like to run, use the treadmill, lift, play basketball," he says. "In this business you can get stressed out; it can be very demanding. So I love to work out to relieve that. Doing the shows really helps too, because you're sweating so much for an hour and a half at a time. Being onstage and getting that energy with the fans, there is an

Relaxing backstage.

Julie Blattberg

opportunity there to forget about all the other nonsense in the business. If you've had a bad day you just get out there and you just kind of forget about it, you feel kind of liberated for an hour and a half. I'm probably in the best shape of my life right now because of it."

If you've been checking out Nick's biceps, you've probably noticed his tattoos. To show their brotherly bond, he and Drew have matching armbands with the family "L" monogram in the middle of it. "We tried to get our dad to get one, too," Drew jokes. "But he wouldn' t go for it."

Nick Lachey

Nick also has a sun design with 98° written in the middle of it. "People always say, 'What if you break up?' but in some way, 98° will always be a great part of my life. Plus, if I really don't like it I could always color the sun in", he jokes. "But seriously, 98° is always something that I will be proud to have been a part of."

In fact, Nick hopes that the group stays together for a long time. "I would like us to be," he says. "I don't think any of us have put any limit on this group at all. I think as long as we enjoy our lives and our careers, we will stick with it. And as long as our fans stick with us, we'll be here. I would like to be performing all my life in one form or another. I think we all have a future in production and writing and I think we'll always be connecting musically."

Nick would love to work with other artists, too, someday, like Boyz II Men or Sade. "I'm a huge Sade fan," he says. "I think she's got one of the most beautiful voices ever, and I would love to sing something with her."

But surprisingly, Nick says his professional role model is not in the music biz. "Bruce Willis is someone I've always looked up to. That guy is incredible. I would love to be like him someday."

"My personal role model is my dad," he says. "I never met a kinder person in my life. He's everything I want to be in my life as a father and a person, and he has really set a great example for Drew and me."

Justin, Jeff, and Drew unanimously voted Nick to be the "intense" member of the group. "I tend to get that way," Nick agrees. "I take things very seriously and I'm one of those types of people who likes to be a leader. I guess I am intense only because I care. I want us to be successful."

He goes on to describe himself as "a type A personality. Everything in my life I approach with a real intense attitude. It can be good and bad; I try to balance it out. The other guys can always count on me to care and be passionate about the group, and that's all I want them to know—that I'm gonna give it my all."

Nick's favorite 98° song reflects that side of him. "It's 'Heaven's Missing An Angel,' from our first album. I like it because it's a very intense—kind of like my personality—and beautiful, emotional song. No words can describe the ones that you love. It's always been my favorite."

His advice to singers who want to make it big also mirrors his driven personality. "Believe in yourself and stay dedicated," he says thoughtfully. "There are people out there who are more talented than I am and who will never make it because they never try. You have to believe in yourself and go out there and give it a try. And stick with it, keep your goals in focus, and work your butt off. There are no free lunches out there. You have to make other people believe in you."

JEFF

51°

JEFFREY "JEFF" BRANDON TIMMONS

BIRTHDATE: April 30, 1973
STAR SIGN: Taurus
BIRTHPLACE: Canton, Ohio
HEIGHT: 5' 8"
WEIGHT: 160 lbs.
HAIR: Brown
EYES: Blue
PARENTS: Trish and Jim
SIBLINGS: Brother Mike, 29; sister Tina, 24
FAVORITE PERFORMERS: Boyz II Men
FAVORITE SONG: "It's So Hard to Say Goodbye to Yesterday" by Boyz II Men
FAVORITE FOODS: Seafood and steak
FAVORITE COLORS: Orange, blue
FAVORITE SPORT: Football
FAVORITE TEAM: Dallas Cowboys
FAVORITE ACTOR: Robert De Niro
FAVORITE ACTRESS: Salma Hayek
FAVORITE MOVIE: *The Shawshank Redemption*
FAVORITE 98° SONG: "Heaven's Missing an Angel"
FAVORITE COLLECTOR'S ITEM: Football cards
FAVORITE CHILDHOOD TOY, ACCORDING TO MOM: A Spider-Man doll

VITAL STATISTICS

"I LIKE A GIRL WITH A NICE SMILE AND GREAT PERSONALITY. A GOOD SENSE OF HUMOR IS ESSENTIAL BECAUSE I'M A SCREW-OFF."

You would think that Jeff Timmons wouldn't have to do much to meet girls, but he claims that he had to start singing to get their attention. "Growing up, I sang a little bit here and there, in choirs," he says. "I was pretty timid, but I did sing in a barbershop quartet in high school. Then I started this group with these guys that I went to high school and college with. Once we were at a party and these girls asked us to sing, so we thought we'd be cool and try to get the girls. We went in the bathroom and started pairing harmonies to 'My Girl.' When we came out and sang it, the girls loved it. I actually didn't know anything about five-part harmony, but I thought, 'I'm gonna quit school now, and I'm gonna get all the girls!'"

And that's exactly what Jeff did. He left Kent State University, and moved out to Los Angeles to make it big.

"He always pursued things like that," his mother, Trish, says. "Actually, when he was in grade

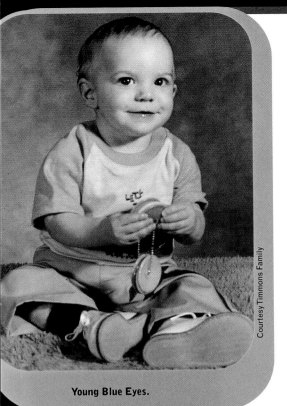

Courtesy Timmons Family

Young Blue Eyes.

knew Jeff was very talented and he had aspirations. I wasn't surprised, and we are very supportive of what our children do because we know they are good people and that you should try to accomplish your goals. If it doesn't work out you can just move on."

Jeff appreciates how supportive his family has been. "They've been great," he says. "My dad originally was like 'college, college, college.' He was always pounding it in our heads to go, and I'm not telling anyone to drop out, but I didn't really fit there. I got decent grades, but I never really excelled. When I dropped out, he did make a big

psychology major, and I wanted to work with children. If I never pursued singing I probably would have ended up a child psychologist or a pediatrician."

Moving out West worked out well for Jeff, whose family was relocating to California, anyway. In fact, his older brother, Mike, was already in Tinseltown pursuing an acting career.

Jeff tried his best to focus on music in L.A. but he did get sidetracked at times. One of his first "performing" gigs was in a commercial for the Navy. "That was a freakish thing," he explains. "I lived in L.A. and my brother and his

"IN HIGH SCHOOL I ENDED UP GETTING KICKED OUT OF CHOIR BECAUSE I WAS ALWAYS GOOFING AROUND. IT'S KIND OF IRONIC."

school he would come home and say, 'I am going to try out for this play and I am going to get the lead.' Throughout junior high, high school, and college, he had participated in local theater and he did a lot of plays. When he was in college and was taking psychology, he told me that he was putting this singing group together, and I said, 'That's great.' And he said, 'No, I am really serious about this.' And he wanted to move out to Los Angeles and start the group there. We were really supportive. We all

stink about it, but he also did say, 'Follow your dream.' My parents have both been our biggest fans."

Although he's melting hearts all over the world with his smooth tenor, Jeff is the first to say that he never really planned on being a performer until he moved to L.A. "I played football at Malone College and I wanted to be a pro player," he says. "But I was nowhere near being good enough for that. That was one dream of mine. I also really wanted to practice law. In college I was a

roommate were trying to pursue acting careers. Now, the thing about L.A. is, all of these people move out there and they want to be actors, but they go out there and party instead of acting. They live the scene, but they don't really take it seriously. They'll pay for all of these elaborate photos and never go on the auditions. My brother's roommate was supposed to go down to this audition, but he instead went to Cancún on a whim, just to hang out and party. One day his manager called for him and I answered the phone and I said he was away. So she said, 'Hey, do you want to go on an audition today?'"

Jeff still laughs, remembering his luck. "I said OK, and I went, but didn't take it too seriously. You were supposed to be represented by an agency, and I lied; I wrote down a fake agency. Then they asked me to turn a certain way, and say certain things. I didn't know what I was doing. I felt like a complete idiot. Then they said, 'OK, we'll let you know.' When I got called back for it, I was on my way to work as a security guard, so I was in uniform. The lady said, 'You've got to come down right now,' and I showed up to the audition with this uniform on, and everyone thought I was trying to be cool. But I ended up getting the job. In the commercial I played a Navy guy and I got to drive a Mustang in Hawaii. I was really lucky. It was a blessing because I needed the money, so I was able to take some time and hook up with the guys and start singing."

Acting in a commercial and working as a security guard were some of the better jobs Jeff has worked in his lifetime. "The worst was when I was a cook in a Chinese restaurant, back when minimum wage was $3.50 an hour," he says.

"I was the new kid there, and they worked my butt off. I washed dishes, bused tables, scrubbed floors, cleaned and also cooked. They had me do everything for $3.50 an hour."

Jeff grew up the middle child of Jim, a corporate vice president, and Trish, a bridal consultant, in the small town of Massillon, Ohio. Unlike the other guys, Jeff didn't go to a performing-arts school or have any particular training in the arts. "I used to act in a lot of different stuff like plays

High school, senior year.

Jeff with his sister Kristina.

and musicals while growing up, but it was more a hobby for me," he says. "I was always in choir and I liked it but I was always scared, I never really sung out. In fact, in high school I ended up getting kicked out of choir because I was always goofing around. It's kind of ironic."

"I think he got his talent from his grandfather, who played the violin," Jeff's mom says. "Jeff played trumpet in high school, and I think he has the same good ear that his grandfather had. But mostly I think he was just blessed with a God-given talent."

Trish describes Jeff as having a great sense of humor. He's always been a clown and he's always been loving. He's funny; he makes you laugh. He has a sense of humor you wouldn't believe."

"The time I truly realized that he had a God-given gift for music was when he tried out for a play at a local theater and he had to sing

54°

Courtesy Troup & Pluto Studios

Courtesy Timmons Family

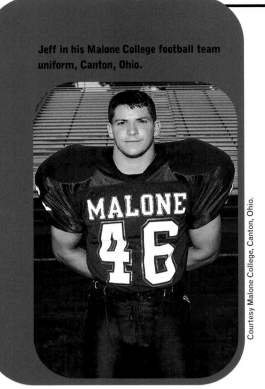

Jeff in his Malone College football team uniform, Canton, Ohio.

O Come, All Ye Faithful,'" Trish reminisces. "I had never really heard him sing before. But he did it so perfectly and so beautifully that everyone was stunned, and I cried. He was only about 12 years old."

That voice would make Jeff famous. "Fame is cool," he says. "You get to meet all kinds of cool people. We get to go to great places, like Southeast Asia, and see different cultures. It's definitely a wonderful thing. But there are some drawbacks," he adds. "Like lack of time with your family. I'm a big family guy. It's really tough when you don't get to see them. I guess I'm a mama's boy and daddy's boy at the same time. My dad coached my football teams growing up and he was always there when I needed him. I'm really close with my brother and sister now, but we used to fight all the time when I was a kid."

Jeff stays in touch with his family nearly every day, and though they don't get to see him much, they enjoy tracking 98°'s success by looking up the band's chart position on the Internet. "I have terrific grandparents, too," Jeff says. "It's hard when you can't see them as often. That is definitely the downside to being famous."

What does Jeff look for in a girl? "I like a girl with a nice smile and great personality. A good sense of humor is essential because I'm a screw-off. I'm always messing around—sometimes too much," he says. "I'm lighthearted and like to enjoy life. I can't be with someone who is too serious, but I also need someone to keep me in line when I need it."

Where would he take a girl for a great date? "I'm kind of a goof, so, one of my favorite restaurants is Denny's," he admits, laughing. "I like the breakfast they have, so I might take her there on a first date. I also like playing pool, hanging out, going to get something to eat, going to see a movie, and just enjoying a girl's company. It doesn't have to be anything special."

Although he likes to keep his dates simple, Jeff has been known to do some pretty elaborate things to get a girl's attention. "I once went on a radio station and got on the air and told them I was in love with some girl," he says. "I used to do all kinds of crazy stuff like that. Another time, this girl I dated in high school was hinting around that she would like it if a guy came and threw rocks at her window to wake her up. She lived in a completely different city, so I walked for two hours early in the morning to throw rocks at her window. But she didn't wake up! Even worse, she called me at 3 in the morning and I wasn't home, because I was walking there, and she thought I was out with another girl or something!"

During the Philippines tour.

"Carpe Diem" - Seize The Day

— Nothing is going to just fall in your lap. You must take full advantage of each day that God Gives you to achieve your goals And dreams, and to live life to the highest of your potential. —

56

Even though Jeff no longer spends his spare time chasing girls, he likes to fill up his downtime hanging out at his apartment

Thumbs up with Justin at Richard Petty's Driving Exprience.

Courtesy THE WALT DISNEY COMPANY.

in Southern California, playing or watching football, collecting "thousands upon thousands" of football cards, lifting weights, and reading. "I like to read at least three books a week," he says. "I like to learn as much as I can."

He's been known to pull his share of pranks during slow time on the road. "I'm the comic relief," he says about his role in the group. "I'm lighthearted, and I think we need that sometimes. Some of the guys are very, very serious about this business, and they should be. But sometimes we need to look at it as this isn't that serious. It's not our health, or our life. I think I add humor to the whole experience."

The other guys agree that Jeff is the most fun-loving, but they are also quick to point out that he is also loyal and dedicated.

"I love each and every aspect of being in 98°," Jeff continues. "I like being on tour, and I like performing. I love being in the studio, putting together songs, writing songs, getting involved with the vocals, and producing, too. That's something I really enjoy."

His favorite 98° song, as well as his mom's, is "Heaven's Missing an Angel." "The song has a lot of meaning to it for me," Jeff confides. "I think it is a beautiful miracle song. The night we recorded it, my grandmother passed away and I wasn't there. She was sick with cancer for quite some time and I had just seen her right before that. But that night she had gone into the hospital and the whole family was there and I wasn't. She was one of my favorite people in the whole world. She was very cool. It was a tough time and the song always brings chills to me." Perhaps that's why he has a tattoo on his chest that says, "Heaven and Good Luck" in addition to the 98° logo on his arm, and the Japanese character for "God" on his back.

Family man Jeff looks to his father as a role model in his personal life. "He served his country in the Army and he was in the Vietnam War," Jeff says. "He came back and has never had a college education, and he's always bettered himself in his jobs. He always worked hard and got promoted, and he is at the top of his business now. And he's given his kids everything. Not one time have I ever been without. He's never been a jerk to anybody. That is amazing to me. People love him, they think he is a great

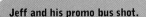

Jeff and his promo bus shot.

Jeff

Johnny Camisa

guy. He's taught us well, too, to be humble and respect people."

Jeff believes it's that influence that helps him stay down-to-earth. "No matter how popular we're getting, we will remain grounded guys. It's not going to change us," he asserts. "We don't want to be catered to because we're singers. Personally, I think everyone has a talent—a particular God-given thing to excel in. Some talents are looked upon differently than others. Someone could be the best carpenter in the world yet he would never get the same recognition that a great actor would get. But he excels way past everyone else. I respect that guy just as much as I respect a famous singer. You're just a person. You put your pants on one leg at a time. I know it's a cliché to say that, but it's true. You live, you breathe, and you're gonna die, so you have to treat everyone else with the same respect with which you want to be treated."

His mother agrees that that philosophy helps Jeff stay the sweet, compassionate person he is. "Onstage I still see that compassion, sensitivity, and strength that he has. He really loves what he is doing, and it shines through."

天吉

Heaven + Good Luck (Blessings)
Things you need to be successful in life!

Julie Blattberg

"I JUST WANT TO HAVE A BUNCH OF KIDS, SETTLE DOWN, AND BE HAPPY. THAT'S WHAT LIFE IS ALL ABOUT ANYWAY."

Down the road, Jeff hopes that he'll still be involved in music, and he would one day like to work with Boyz II Men, Lenny Kravitz, Steve Perry of Journey, or his professional role model, Stevie Wonder, once again. "He inspires me because he has overcome a disability and become super successful."

To aspiring singers, Jeff says, "Sing for anyone who will listen. Have faith, stay humble no matter what, and don't believe any negatives people tell you. People will tell you anything to get you to not follow your dream because they don't have the guts to follow theirs. Believe in what you believe in.

"You never know what the future holds," he goes on. "I hope we can keep on being creative and hopefully get our music out there as long as we like to do it. I also would really like a large family, and if this doesn't work out I would like to be coaching football or teaching kids in high school, like math, or something so I can be with my family. I just want to have a bunch of kids, settle down, and be happy. That's what life is all about anyway."

MOST EMBARRASSING MOMENTS

ONSTAGE:

"There are so many; it's a daily occurrence with me. We were in Toronto, and there was a girl in the audience whom I was looking at and trying to sing to, and be cool and stuff, and I was backing up. I backed up over one of the wedges the guitar player had on the floor, and I fell and landed headfirst on stage. My microphone flew out into the audience, and my headphones came off. It was a disaster! I thought I would have heard dead silence from the audience, but I heard roaring laughter. Nobody cared about my health....They just laughed!

"Another time were doing this thing for the NFL and United Way, and Jerry Rice was there, and we were all on risers. I was standing on one that was one height and he was on one a couple of feet behind me. I turned around and stuck my hand out and said, 'Hey, Jerry, what's up!' and stepped to the right and there was no riser there. I fell off the stage and everyone started laughing. That was my most embarrassing moment ever, probably."

OFFSTAGE:

"When I was a kid we lived by this field and there were houses being built behind us. I used to hang out with this kid who lived a block away and I used to go through the fields to his house. One time there was this huge storm and my dad called and told me to come home. So I ran across the field in mud that was like quicksand. I fell in the mud and got stuck in it up to my chest, and I was screaming, 'Dad! Somebody help me!' I was stuck in the mud and I thought I was gonna die. My neighbor came out and pulled me out with a big branch and saved my life. It was just like in the movies. When I got home my mom pulled my dad out of the shower so he could see me. My father had been looking out the window, watching me struggle and cracking up!"

Johnny Camisa

In London for the "Smash Hits" tour.

HEATING UP THE SCENE

SPENDING THE DAY WITH 98°

Jeff, Nick, Drew, and Justin all agree that life on the road isn't easy. When they aren't onstage, they are giving interviews, doing signings, meeting their fans, recording, or rehearsing. Their hectic schedule is exhausting, but these four fellows handle it like the pros they are. Here's the itinerary from their recent visit to New York City.

Outside in Times Square the fans are screaming and the guys turn around to wave.

Julie Blattberg

4:15 AM After a sensational show and only three hours' sleep, the guys wake up and meet, to make their way to the airport in Grand Rapids, Michigan to catch a flight to New York for their next gig.

6:15 AM The guys are at the airport on time, but the early morning fog causes a delay. They miss their connection, but land in New York just in time for their first appointment of the day.

12:30 PM A van picks up the fab four at Newark Airport and they are whisked to their hotel to drop off their bags. There's no time for lunch, and because of the delay, the guys don't have much time to dally.

Croonin' the tunes.

Julie Blattberg

1:45 PM 98° arrives at MTV to prepare for a performance for *Total Request Live*. Nick sports a Los Angeles Dodgers baseball jersey and jeans. Jeff is comfortable in a sweater and dark pants. Drew wears his trademark backward baseball cap, a ski vest, and baggy khakis. Justin chills in a baby-blue V-neck, which matches his eyes, and comfortable light slacks. In the green room, the producer preps the guys for what will happen on the show. Finally, lunch is delivered from Virgil's, a local southern-style barbecue restaurant. The guys barely have time to dig in to the chicken, ribs, mashed potatoes, rice, and collard greens.

2:10 PM Drew, Nick, Jeff, and Justin are called in for soundcheck in the studio overlooking Times Square. Already fans line the streets outside, even though it's raining. They shake homemade signs declaring their love for the quartet. Some girls have "98" emblazoned on T-shirts; others have painted the logo on their faces. Their shrieks are so loud they can be heard through the glass window of the second-story studio. The group walks to the windows and delights the fans by waving before they take their places on stools and sing "The Hardest Thing" for the soundcheck.

Julie Blattberg

Inside the *Total Request Live* studio, the sound check is underway. Check out the guys' color coded microphones.

2:30 PM It's time for makeup and hairstyling, and the guys disappear into their dressing rooms. They emerge in all black with silver neck chains to dress up the elegant look.

3:10 PM All spruced up, Justin, Jeff, Drew, and Nick do an MTV Radio interview and pose for online photos.

Julie Blattberg

Time for the real show. The live audience can't believe Jeff, Justin, Drew, and Nick are right in front of them.

3:30 PM *Total Request Live* with host Dave Holmes hits the air. The studio audience is buzzing with excitement to see their favorite foursome perform. The crowd outside has grown, and the screams become more frantic as Dave starts the countdown of MTV's most requested videos of the day. Helping him is new VJ sensation Thalia, and actor Scott Foley of *Felicity*.

Jeff solos while Justin, Nick and Drew harmonize, then it's time for the lucky winners in the studio audience to receive their gift CDs right from the guys.

Julie Blattberg

3:55 PM It's time to introduce the No. 3 requested video of the day, which is none other than "The Hardest Thing" by 98°. Jeff, Drew, Justin, and Nick enter the studio, and the crowds—inside and outside—go wild. The guys chat with Dave, and take a question from the audience. They shake hands with the audience members during the commercial break.

4:00 PM 98° performs an exquisite live version of their megahit "The Hardest Thing." The music drops away at the end, leaving the guys to finish it off with their amazing a cappella harmonies. Meanwhile, MTV has picked four fans from outside to come into the studio. They can hardly contain themselves as the group hands them each a 98° CD after the performance. Dave announces that inside one of the CDs is a free pair of tickets for the 98° concert the next evening. The lucky winner is ecstatic as she proudly gets her picture taken with the guys.

The guys pose for their fans at a local CD retailer.

Julie Blattberg

Fans were lined up at 6:30 a.m. to catch their favorite band.

68°

4:10 PM Thalia asks the guys how she should cope with her newfound fame. The guys give her tips on how to keep it real, then introduce a Ricky Martin video.

4:20 PM 98° finishes their part on *Total Request Live*. They have ten minutes to relax before their next appearance.

4:30 PM The group piles into the van again (no limos for these simple guys). Their destination: Macy's for a fashion show sponsored by *YM* magazine and WKTU radio. Fans already mob the store. A lucky 500 of them receive passes to see the guys perform after the fashion show.

At Macy's the group sings again, and meets more screaming fans.

5:00 PM Drew, Jeff, Nick, and Justin enjoy the fashion show and prepare for their performance.

Julie Blattberg

6:00 PM The group performs their hits "Because of You" and "The Hardest Thing."

6:30 PM The fans who hold passes get to meet and greet the group as they sign photos and CDs for the next hour. The guys truly enjoy meeting the fans and graciously accept their gifts of flowers, stuffed animals, cards, photos, and letters.

7:45 PM No time for rest! The band is in the van again, this time headed for a live on-air interview at one of the top radio stations in the New York area.

8:15–9:00 PM 98° arrives at the station and spends 45 minutes on the popular *Night Show*. They sing a dazzling a cappella version of "The Hardest Thing" for listeners.

10:00 PM The guys reach their Manhattan hotel, where after a hard—and long—day's work, they can enjoy a late dinner and then crash. Tomorrow is an even busier day: They will be taping two episodes of the soap *As the World Turns*, signing CDs at a record store, meeting contest winners, officially receiving their platinum plaque from Mel Lewinter, the head of their label Universal, doing television interviews, and performing a concert!

72°

Julie Blattberg

"THE FANS ARE THE BACKBONE OF ANY GROUP. WE HAVE SOME OF THE BEST FANS IN THE WORLD. THEY HAVE BEEN 100% SUPPORTIVE OF US, AND HAVE ALWAYS BEEN THERE TO MAKE US FEEL WELCOME. THANK YOU FOR ALWAYS BEING THERE AND THANK YOU FOR ALWAYS APPRECIATING WHAT WE DO. AS LONG AS WE HAVE FANS, AS LONG AS WE HAVE A CAREER, WE'LL KEEP DOING WHAT WE DO, AND HOPEFULLY EVERYONE WILL CONTINUE TO ENJOY IT WITH US."—NICK "THANKS FOR ALL THE LOVE AND SUPPORT. WE HOPE YOU ALL KNOW WHAT IT HAS MEANT TO US, AND WE WISH YOU ALL THE BEST. WE HOPE YOU ALL FOLLOW YOUR DREAMS, AND WE WISH WE COULD MAKE THEM COME TRUE, LIKE YOU MADE OURS COME TRUE."—JUSTIN "I WANT TO THANK AND BLESS ALL OF OUR FANS. OF COURSE WITHOUT YOU GUYS 98° WOULDN'T BE HERE AND WE APPRECIATE THE SUPPORT. IF WE COULD MEET AND TALK TO EVERY ONE OF YOU, WE WOULD. BUT WHILE WE CAN'T DO THAT, OUR BLESSINGS AND OUR THOUGHTS ARE WITH YOU ALWAYS."—JEFF "WE LOVE OUR FANS AND WE REALIZE WE WOULD HAVE NO CAREER WITHOUT YOU. WE HOPE WE CAN CONTINUE TO MAKE MUSIC THAT YOU EMBRACE AND APPRECIATE. WE THANK ALL OF YOU."—DREW

Johnny Camisa

eff, Drew, Nick, and Justin all agree that they have the best fans in the world, and they continue to be amazed at the reactions they get at each performance.

Nick describes seeing a sea of screaming fans as an awesome experience. "It's such a surreal sight to see, and we can't believe it's for us. It's the ultimate gratification to see fans appreciate our work and our efforts, and to be supportive like that."

"It is very exciting and a great rush," Justin agrees. "We feel so fortunate to have the fans that we do, and that there are so many and they are so enthusiastic. Even if you have a bad night, you still feel good about how the audience reacted to the show."

"For me it's an adrenaline rush," Drew says. "To just go out there and see the girls screaming, that's one of the biggest perks of the job for me."

"I used to be very nervous when I performed," Jeff says. "When we first started performing,

Julie Blattberg

Johnny Camisa

all over the world. There are fans whom I feel like I know pretty well at this point. I have extensive telephone conversations with some. I knew the guys would be appreciated for their music, but the number of people whom their music has really touched and changed their lives in some ways was just not something I had thought about. Some of the letters we get are from people who say a song got them through a really horrible time, and they really feel like they are only making it through now because of the guys."

"A letter from someone explaining how you touched them is the best thing you can get from a fan," Nick says. "One fan's father got sick with cancer and she said there is this song on our album that meant a lot to both of them and it has helped her since he died. Something like that really makes what we do worthwhile."

Nick goes on, "There was a little boy whose foster mother wrote in saying he had been abused and had become completely noncommunicative. He hadn't talked, written, or anything. But then he became interested in us as a group and learned to read the liner notes on the CD. Since then he put together a scrapbook for us and learned

we used to do a show every night, and I used to get sick—physically ill—before I would go onstage. But now it's like second nature, and it's a blast, and I think it's mostly because of the fan reaction. Not only do we have screaming girls out there, we have women and men in their thirties and forties. To see all those people singing the songs we sing is amazing."

No one is more amazed at the 98° fans than the group's mothers. "I think it's really cute," Justin's mother says. "The first time I saw that was when I flew to Chicago and they sang in the pouring rain. The fans were still hanging in there. I noticed the way Justin really talked to them

on a friendly, intimate level."

"It just takes my breath away," says Jeff's mother. "I remember it was like the Beatles. It's just a wonderful experience for me to see people get excited like that about my son."

"I just want to laugh sometimes," Nick and Drew's mom, Cate, says. "Girls get hysterical if they get their picture taken with me and I am just a mom of these regular guys! I know that they are all just regular guys, and great guys—all four of them."

Cate enjoys the fans so much that she is the president of the official 98° fan club. "My husband and I, in our spare time, run the club," she explains. "We get hundreds of letters a day from

Julie Blattberg

how to write. She told us that we were responsible for completely changing him as a person. We actually got to meet him a few months ago in Florida. To know you've touched a life is awesome. A lot of people in this business don't understand that we have an opportunity to touch a lot of people, and a lot of people abuse that, or don't take the opportunity."

Justin agrees. "The greatest part about performing is that we can touch people's hearts, souls, and lives. Everybody goes through hard times—especially when you're younger and going through teenage years. Things can be tough in school. It's nice to be a positive influence."

This socially minded vocal group even started a foundation to help charities and fans with special needs. "We work with a lot of groups and charities," manager Paris D'Jon explains. "They'll do anything and everything. We've done a coat drive, and a Christmas tree drive. We've worked with the Boys Club, Girls Club, Habitat for Humanity. We donate tickets for every show to handicapped people, kids with AIDS or leukemia, the Make-A-Wish Foundation, and many others."

Johnny Camisa

"THE GREATEST PART ABOUT PERFORMING IS THAT WE CA TOUCH PEOPLE'S HEARTS, SOULS, AND LIVES

It's not surprising that these gorgeous, talented, and good-hearted guys have such a loyal fan base. And it's even less surprising that some fans have done crazy things to get close to the guys and get their attention.

"They call me," Justin's mom says. "Most of the time they'll just ask, 'Is this Justin with 98°'s house?' and I just say, 'Can I take a message?' One time I got a call from a girl in the Philippines. I arranged for her to call when Justin would be here. I figured if she's calling all the

Julie Blattberg

FANS WILL ALSO MOB THE TOUR BUS AND PUT LIPSTICK KISS MARKS ALL OVER IT, STEAL THE GUYS' WATER BOTTLES FROM THE STAGE AND EVEN HIDE IN LAUNDRY BASKETS IN HOTELS TO GET IN THEIR ROOMS!

way from the Philippines that he should talk to her."

"We have changed our phone number already," Jeff's mother says. "And they send gifts here. However, it's sweet. It hasn't been too bad for us."

"We have a lot of fans who try to jump onstage," says Thomas Lee, the 98° head of security. "We have girls in the hotels who try to sleep outside their doors. There are girls who try to rip away their clothes all the time."

"They've flashed us, thrown undergarments on stage," Justin adds. "We have some fans who have 98° tattoos. Sometimes a fan will make food for you. And we've gotten pet turtles, which was cool, but unfortunately we couldn't keep them."

Fans will also mob the tour bus and put lipstick kiss marks all over it, steal the guys' water bottles from the stage, and even hide in laundry baskets in hotels to get in their rooms!

"I've even heard of girls staying overnight for three days in the rain just to get tickets," Paris says. "But it's all because they are the most loyal, dedicated fans I've ever seen."

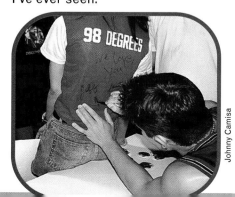

Johnny Camisa

Johnny Camisa

Wrapping the bus.

98° has one of the hottest stage shows in the music business, and that's because the guys work hard at it. Before they start a tour, they work with their choreographer, Lea Dellecave, for weeks. She will even go to some of the shows when the guys take the act on the road and offer feedback after each performance.

You won't see 98° singing along to a prerecorded backtrack. "We have some of the best musicians I have ever heard," says Justin. "We are very excited to be working with them. They are just great guys, too. Sometimes when you are working with musicians at that level, as talented as they really are, egos come into play. But these guys are all real cool, they have a lot of experience on tour, and they just know how to have fun when it is time to play."

"They are basically the hottest band in the country," manager Paris D'Jon agrees. "They have played with everyone from Mary J. Blige to Boyz II Men."

"Drew, Nick, Justin, and Jeff can really sing," says Kenny Seymour, the musical director. "They have terrific voices, they are very professional, and they are terrific guys. We all hang out together offstage, too, and do fun things like play laser tag. There's a real family feeling among all of us."

Net. And it plays CDs. That's probably my favorite thing," Jeff confides.

"I always take my camera with me, in case I meet somebody, or take a picture if I'm someplace really cool," Drew says. "I also take my CD collection, and my Sony Playstation."

"I bring favorite movies, CDs, video games, and I just got a

computer, so I think I will take that with me," Nick says. "You try to limit what you take because you know eventually you will have to carry it somewhere. But you try to bring as much as you can to make it feel like home."

"We take things that we need, like clothes and stuff, and I bring my sunglasses, books, and CDs," Justin says. "If you've got a lot

It's great playing with these guys, it's wonderful," guitarist Ric Molina agrees. "It's interesting to be in the vortex of all this attention. We come out of the venue and the girls tell us how much they love us and everything, which is very funny because we all have families and wives or girlfriends."

When they embark on a tour, there are certain things the fab four never leave home without. "I just got a laptop PC and I can e-mail people now, or get on the

to think about it's great to bury your head in a book or listen to a great CD."

The guys pack it all in a huge tour bus that Drew says is "a little too posh for us. It has leather seats and nice woodwork and a great shower. There's a satellite TV, which we can watch sports on, and a full-size fridge. It has ten bunks, six regular, plus the

four double-size that we get. It's real nice, but sometimes it's hard to relax because it's *too* nice."

Those are much better digs than the bus the group started out with. "They had thirteen of us on this old bus, rolling through Canada," Ric Molina remembers. "But the bus only slept twelve, so someone had to sleep up front. It was so dry on that bus that we got this humidifier. The humidifier was huge, and was supposed to be used for very large rooms. We'd turn that thing on and everybody would end up in a huge sweat. And every time you put on the brakes, the water would sprinkle out onto the carpet. So in the morning we'd get up and all thirteen of us would have one sock that was wet. The heat was unregulated, so in the front you'd be freezing, in the back you'd be burning up, and in the bunks it would be raining."

But getting there is only half the fun, according to the guys. They say performing is the best part of the job. And to do that, they'll get there any way they can.

Johnny Camisa

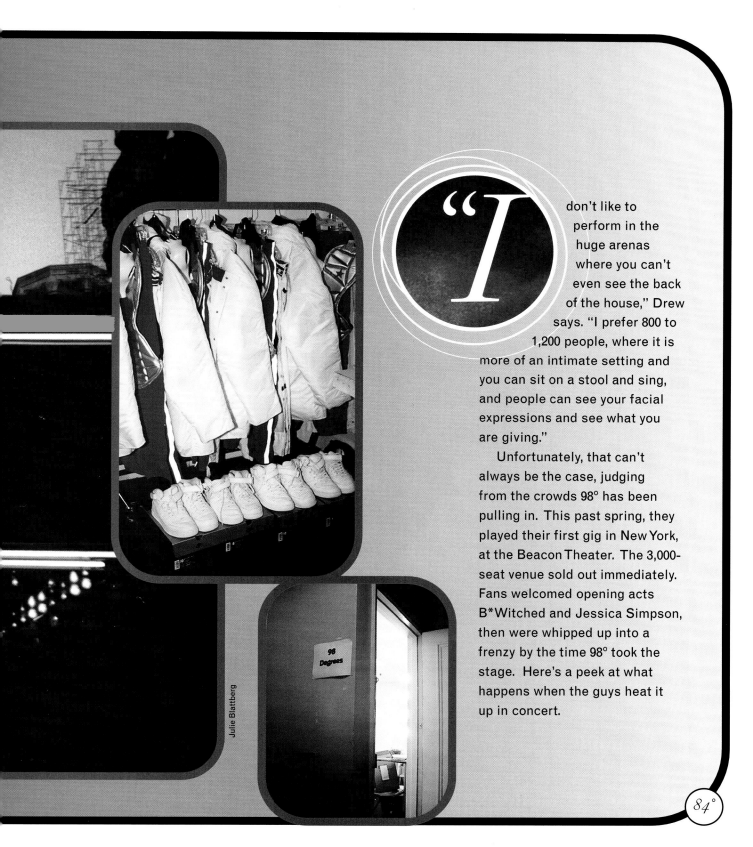

Julie Blattberg

"*I* don't like to perform in the huge arenas where you can't even see the back of the house," Drew says. "I prefer 800 to 1,200 people, where it is more of an intimate setting and you can sit on a stool and sing, and people can see your facial expressions and see what you are giving."

Unfortunately, that can't always be the case, judging from the crowds 98° has been pulling in. This past spring, they played their first gig in New York, at the Beacon Theater. The 3,000-seat venue sold out immediately. Fans welcomed opening acts B*Witched and Jessica Simpson, then were whipped up into a frenzy by the time 98° took the stage. Here's a peek at what happens when the guys heat it up in concert.

Julie Blattberg

"Before every show we get together, the band, wardrobe, security—everyone— and we hold hands, say a prayer thanking God for our blessings and asking for his continued strength and guidance," Drew explains. "Then just the four of us will get in a huddle and put our hands in the middle. It really helps us to stay focused and all be on the same page." The night at the Beacon was no exception.

The stage set features a huge 98° logo mounted in the center. Two staircases reach a catwalk, which runs across the stage.

The opera *Carmina Burana* blares through the speakers, signaling the start of the show.

Julie Blattberg

"BEFORE EVERY SHOW **WE GET TOGETHER**, THE BAND, WARDROBE, SECURITY— EVERYONE—AND WE HOLD HANDS, SAY A **PRAYER** THANKING GOD FOR OUR **BLESSINGS** AND ASKING FOR CONTINUED **STRENGTH** AND **GUIDANCE**."

Julie Blattberg

Julie Blattberg

86°

Four *Star Trek*-style booths light up. As a mysterious fog fills the stage, a deep, omniscient voice introduces Jeff, Justin, Nick, and Drew. Four beings dressed in white spacesuit-like costumes and masks step out of the booths and onto the stage.

The smoke lifts while a heartbeat pulses throughout the arena, getting louder and louder. The temperature rises. The shrieks of the fans grow wild with the anticipation of seeing their four favorite singers burst into action.

Suddenly, the guys whip off the masks and peel off the spacesuits. Underneath, it's Jeff, Justin, Drew, and Nick in red track pants and silver breast-plates, gladiator-style. The crowd whips into a frenzy as they kick off the show with "Heat It Up," the theme song of the tour.

They follow with "Fly With Me" and stop the song near the end when Jeff bursts into a wacky funky-chicken dance routine. Then the guys segue into the Offspring's popular tune, "Pretty Fly (For A White Guy)."

The guys take it up a notch for a rendition of Prince's timely tune, "1999." The crowd chants "Party!" as the foursome runs backstage for a quick change.

Julie Blattberg

Julie Blattberg

89°

Julie Blattberg

Julie Blattberg

The band plays on, and just as the audience becomes antsy waiting for 98° to reappear, Jeff, Nick, Drew, and Justin rise up from the catwalk in elegant black suits with valentine-red shirts underneath. They sport this suave style for "Invisible Man" and "I Do (Cherish You)," which Nick dedicates to "anyone who's ever been in love in New York City."

Drew heats things up when he starts "Do You Wanna Dance." Justin dons his trademark shades as he asks the title question in his booming bass.

Next thing you know, the guys are grooving again, as they put their mikes into stands and sing Stevie Wonder's "Superstition"

brings another onstage, sporting the same combat look. Nick and Jeff draw screams from the audience when they come out: they are shirtless under their vests!

Julie Blattberg

amazing group as the lights come up.

As the guys exit the stage, fans shout for an encore while tossing roses and stuffed animals onto

"DO YOU WANNA DANCE?"

Motown-style. They finish it off with a gorgeous a cappella interlude, then introduce their band: Kenny Seymour on keyboards, William Johnson III on drums, Kirk Lyons on bass, and Ric Molina on guitar.

Justin surprises everyone when he comes back onstage, in camouflage pants and a black vest playing the harmonica Stevie Wonder-style. It's time to introduce 98°, and one by one, each member

The foursome breaks into a favorite song, "True to Your Heart," then slows the pace a bit for a medley of some soulful songs including, "If She Only Knew," the oldie "You Are Everything," and the Temptations' "Can't Get Next to You."

The show is so dazzling that it flies by. When the boys croon "The Hardest Thing," the audience sings out every word. The hardest thing is to say good night to this

the stage. They shriek as the lights go out again and the group returns in baby-blue basketball gear to perform their last song of the night, "Because of You." Nick dedicates the hit to all their fans.

The guys hold out their mikes, encouraging the audience to sing along, then seemingly sink magically into the catwalk for their final exit. It's the perfect end to the perfect show, and a night that 98° fans won't ever forget.

Julie Blattberg

Julie Blattberg

94°

95°

Julie Blattberg

Julie Blattberg

Stay in touch with the fabulous foursome, or find out how you can help the 98° Foundation by writing to them at:

98° Worldwide Fan Club
P.O. Box 31379
Cincinnati, OH 45231
Fan Club hot line:
(513) 522-8598

To join their official fan club, send your name, address, birthdate, phone number, and a check or money order for $21.98 ($22.98 Canada, $24.98 international) to the same address. Members will receive an autographed picture, a welcome letter from the guys, a poster, a sticker, a press-on tattoo, an official fan club membership card, and a newsletter four times a year that features articles written by 98° themselves.

You can also visit Nick, Drew, Jeff, and Justin on the Web at their official site:
www.98degrees.com.

Courtesy THE WALT DISNEY COMPANY

PICK UP THESE GREAT 98° TITLES

Nick, Drew, Justin, and Jeff take you backstage, on the road and behind the scenes to give you a glimpse of their lives on the Heat It Up tour. Los Angeles, Bangkok, Canada, Las Vegas, London, Thailand... travel the world with the guys and see what life on the road with 98 Degrees is really about! See the fans, visit a video shoot, a photo shoot, a recording session, TV appearances, concerts and more!

Plus hear the guys as they each tell you their stories about how they met, what their lives are like now, meeting their fans and making music. Everything you need to know about the Ohio foursome! And you'll get the inside scoop on how they make their fantastic videos!

TOTAL RUNNING TIME: 62 MINUTES

UNIVERSAL
RECORDS
A UNIVERSAL MUSIC COMPANY

INSIDE

Invisible Man
Directed By David Nelson

True To Your Heart
Directed By Frederico Tio

Because of You
Directed By Wayne Isham

Was It Something I Didn't Say
Directed By Darren Grant

The Hardest Thing
Directed By Wayne Isham

Heat It Up
(Live at the Wiltern Theater Los Angeles)
Directed By Lee Brownstein - Space Monkey Films

MANAGEMENT:
Paris D'Jon for Top 40 Entertainment
WORLDWIDE FAN CLUB:
P.O. Box 31379, Cincinnati, OH 31379
(513) 522-8598
EXECUTIVE PRODUCER: Paris D'Jon
"KING OF ALL VIDEOS": Jeff Panzer
PROJECT MANAGER: Erin Yasgar

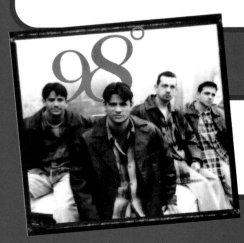

CERTIFIED GOLD DEBUT ALBUM. INCLUDES "INVISIBLE MAN."

FROM UNIVERSAL RECORDS!

98° BRINGS YOU THE CLASSIC CHRISTMAS SONGS PLUS ORIGINAL HOLIDAY TUNES

MULTI-PLATINUM ALBUM INCLUDES THE HITS "BECAUSE OF YOU," "THE HARDEST THING," AND "I DO (CHERISH YOU)."

Bullying.
Threats.
Bullets.

Locker searches? Metal detectors?

Fight back without fists.

MTV's Fight For Your Rights: Take A Stand Against Violence can give you the power to find your own solutions to youth violence. Find out how you can take a stand in your community at FightForYourRights.MTV.com.

fight for your rights:
take a stand against violence